Une Awakenings

Navigating a
Spiritual Awakening

SHARNA LANGLAIS

Samantha Bishop   Juliet Erickson   Rose Gibson
Katy Hughes   Lynn Kay   Lauren Lenore
JR MacGregor   Beverly McDonald Jennifer Nevarez
Caroline Smith   J. Whitley

"It doesn't happen all at once," said the Skin Horse. "You become. It takes a long time. That's why it doesn't happen often to people who break easily, or have sharp edges, or who have to be carefully kept. Generally, by the time you are Real, most of your hair has been loved off, and your eyes drop out and you get loose in the joints and very shabby. But these things don't matter at all, because once you are Real you can't be ugly, except to people who don't understand."

— Margery Williams Bianco, *The Velveteen Rabbit*

DEDICATION

Becoming is an awkward thing. Awakening is harder still.

This book is for the seekers and the journeyers, the old souls in new bodies, the wise ones just learning to own their wisdom, the truth tellers who have been told to keep quiet.

This book is for both the outsiders who have spent their whole lives looking in, in addition to the insiders who have suddenly found themselves on the outside.

It's for anyone who is looking for truth, and has found that the old truths simply no longer work.

To those of you reading this, we say:

You are not alone.

You are in an infinite process of becoming.

Stand tall and don't turn back.

Fall into the arms of these words and let our stories give you strength.

Your bravery is luminous and it is your courage that lights the way.

CONTENTS

PART 3: TOOLS FOR NAVIGATING AN UNEXPECTED AWAKENING

INTRODUCTION

Sunlight peaks through the curtains and washes the couch in a long swath of golden, sunny light. The couch beneath me is springy with movement as I reach for a tissue to hand to the sobbing woman sitting across from me. I feel waves of despair and anguish washing over her, making their way slowly to me. I want to reach out and touch her knee, but I know that she doesn't want to be touched. And so I sit and hold space as I wait for the tears to subside, and she is ready to share.

"There's something wrong with me," she exhales between sobs. "Why doesn't my life work anymore? Everything seems to be falling apart around me, and no matter what I try to do, nothing works. My career, relationships, family and friendships: nothing seems to be what it was, and I'm not even sure I want it to be anyway. But no one around me seems to understand why I can't just be my happy, old self anymore. I feel so alone."

This is the moment, like so many other similar moments, that I wish I could have reached for the book you're holding right now. This is one of dozens of conversations I've had over the last several years that all have the same texture, the same words, the same undertones and context.

I know exactly what to say to my client, in part because it's become almost a ritual of the words that inspired this book. I'll explain the spiritual awakening process, trying my best to convey how many others have journeyed through exactly these experiences. We'll talk about tools to incorporate into the beginnings of this new life, to help him or her find a way forward.

This is also the time that I know my client is barely listening, only halfway able to take in all the information due to the massive level of overwhelm that comes from navigating the awakening process. I know that, during this stage, it's less about the words and more about my tone, more about the in-person reassurance of sitting next to someone who both understands and seems to be able to chart a way forward. I also know that, upon returning home, my client will start to sort through the resources we'd discussed, trying to remember what I had said about others who have gone through this process. She or he will look for the explanation of the awakening process that escapes memory in the blur of everything that has happened before, during, and after our session.

Seeing forward into that moment that almost always comes, I wish I could send my client home with this book. It's from this somewhat self-serving place that this book was born. My initial idea for a resource to help my clients through their awakening process has become so very much more than I ever expected.

This book is by no means an exhaustive overview of the awakening process, and by its very nature, it's also subjective: as each individual awakens in his or her own unique and varied way. Over the course of many personal awakenings of my own, as well as helping others navigate their experiences, I've noticed there are many trends and similarities which the literature on the awakening experience also supports.

Parts One and Three help give more context about the awakening process itself, along with tools and tips to help you navigate through your journey, whatever stage you may find yourself in. And UnexpectedAwakenings.com has been developed to provide additional resources, that we'll be adding to on an ongoing basis, to offer continued support.

The true wealth of information here comes from the eleven personal narratives you'll read in Part Two, bravely shared by my clients and students. They are not meant to be compared to your process, but instead, to provide an example of how various types of awakenings can look and occur. Our deepest hope is that they give you a sense of comfort and strength, the opportunity to perhaps learn from their experience, and also that you find a way forward that works for you.

As Dr. Clarissa Pinkola Estés writes: "Stories are medicine.[1]" We hope you find some medicine on these pages.

PART 1: ABOUT AWAKENINGS

CHAPTER 1

TWO TYPES OF AWAKENING

I have discovered that there are two kinds of awakenings. The first is embarked upon purposefully from a sense that there is something not quite right in one's life; that there is more to the meaning of life, and it lies somewhere on the other side of a spiritual path. Thus, the individual embarks on a journey of spiritual discovery where each step of the awakening process is purposeful and expected, with guides and teachers who are ready and available to assist.

The second kind is what this book is mainly about, what I would call a *spontaneous* or an *unexpected* awakening: life events intercede and wreak their own simultaneously beautiful and horrific havoc, propelling us forward into a rebirth. While many authors have written about the first type of more traditional spiritual awakening, I've found that very little exists to help those in the midst of an unexpected awakening. Specifically, I've found very few resources to help individuals maneuver through it, especially when the awakening feels and looks like a red-alert, catastrophic nightmare of a perfect storm.

One of the most potentially challenging aspects of the awakening experience isn't necessarily the pain and disruption it can create in our lives. Instead, the biggest challenge is the sense of isolation we feel, as everything we once thought we were certain about is ripped out from underneath us. Because we each experience life through our own unique tapestry of beliefs based on the individualized threads that have woven themselves into our lives, we can find ourselves not only uncertain of how to proceed, but where to turn. By its very nature, an awakening means that what once felt comforting and helpful, no longer does.

The term *awakening* describes how our eyes become open to aspects of the world we had not seen before, and also, to an entirely new and often daunting dawn. For most of us, undergoing an awakening is not like waking up in a warm, soft bed, stretching our arms to the sky as the sun gently kisses our faces and we lovingly wipe the sleep from our eyes. Instead, undergoing an awakening can feel like a bucket of ice cold water being dumped all over our naked bodies in the stark cold wilderness where we've been left, quite rudely and unexpectedly, without a compass, supplies, map, or destination. It is the startling-ness of this process that creates the deepest awakening. What we thought we knew and understood about ourselves and the world is ripped away and we are left to wander, trying to put pieces back together that simply won't fit. The awakening process demands that we find new pieces, new patterns, and a new way forward.

It is not surprising that a crisis is often an awakening in disguise.

Traditional Mystical Awakening

In *Kundalini Rising*, Dr. Dorothy Walters discusses the stages of the awakening process based on research into both Eastern and Western religious philosophies. This process is typically sought out purposefully by the individual who is seeking deeper communion with the divine. She outlines the traditional Western (i.e. Christian-based religions) Mystic Path in three stages[2]:

1. Purgation
2. Illumination
3. Union

She notes that Evelyn Underhill instead describes five stages of mystic progression in her work *Mysticism*[3]:

1. **Awakening or conversion:** The understanding that there's a greater spiritual or divine order.
2. **Self-knowledge or purgation:** The recognition that the human experience and the self are necessarily imperfect, especially when contrasted with the divine.
3. **Illumination:** After the process of purging, there is a deeper journey toward the divine in an effort to understand its true nature by releasing attachment. This includes the experience of joy and peace. For many, this is the end of the mystical journey and they go no further.
4. **Surrender or the Dark Night:** St. John referred to The Dark Night of the Soul as a discharging of the superficial joys of transcendence by releasing the ego and attachment completely[4]. As a result, one feels totally alone and even abandoned by the divine.
5. **Union:** the seeker reaches true illumination, and merges with it.

Underhill is also careful to note that, much like the process of grief, these stages are not linear. We may experience these stages cyclically, out of order, or several at the same time. These stages are used to describe the awakening that occurs on the mystic's path, particularly when one intentionally sets out in search of deeper spiritual meaning.

Unexpected Awakenings

For many, the unexpected awakening process is not entirely purposeful. We may possess an awareness that certain aspects of our lives no longer function, or we may feel a sense of emptiness, an undeniable need to search for more. We may already be living a spiritual lifestyle of some type, have a deep sense of faith in the divine, or have pursued personal development work. Since most of us are likely living a secular life, work, family, and other commitments add twists and turns to our spiritual path. As such, we usually can't enter into the same level of immersion required for the traditional mystic. Instead of embarking on a purposeful awakening with the understanding of exactly what such an undertaking includes, it's the circumstances that arise in our lives that propel us through the eye of the needle, usually as hesitant and/or unwilling participants.

In my experience with unexpected awakenings, I see two key components at work that reveal themselves as the genesis of this type of awakening experience:

1.) **External event(s) that force a coming to terms with old ways of being and doing that no longer work.** I see these most often as events of transition including job/career change, pursuing a new learning path, a divorce or break-up, addiction, life-or-death experiences, a new relationship, geographic move/travel, health obstacles/illness, etc. These types of events are likely difficult or challenging in nature, as transitions often are. I've also found that our degree of attachment to control, in addition to how deeply-seeded old patterns and beliefs are in the psyche, are often a direct reflection of how unpleasant that process can be. Often, the

4

stronger or more stubborn one is, the more challenges the universe gives you to induce surrender or shift.

2.) **An internal commitment to self and growth.** This may not be conscious at first. We are often preoccupied with simply surviving or resolving these external events. A commitment to self and growth, however, usually begins when it becomes obvious that old ways of living and being in the world simply aren't going to work anymore. We realize the old tools we had to navigate crisis aren't the right tools anymore. We decide that we don't just want to survive or fix the crisis, we want something better on the other side of it - almost always that *something better* is centered around a better version of ourselves (whether or not we know it at the time). So, we set out trying to figure out how to navigate life in a new way. Committing to this path is key – I haven't seen individuals successfully navigate an awakening without a conscious commitment to self-growth at some point.

It also bears mentioning that, if we truly reflect on the full span of our lives, most of us have had many awakening experiences, many points of crisis or transition, that forced us into new ways of being. Once we have chosen to awaken, we also begin to make sense of transition as a gift to embrace rather than a burden we feel forced to endure. We begin to see these transitional moments as the catalysts of a never-ending process of awakening. They also no longer feel like crises; and while it's human to moan and groan a bit as we grow, once we finish with the initial grumbling, those who have been awakening for many years roll up their sleeves and get to work quite quickly. We embrace the challenge or transition, find the balance between action and surrender, and flow into the dance of shift.

The stories within this book represent the initial awakening moments: the key experience out of many moments in each contributor's life that they define as the most significant springboard from which they jumped into an entirely new way of showing up. These experiences forced them to become fully present to their growth and transformation, and to see it as an ongoing path rather than a singular hurdle to surpass.

I write about an awakening as a process for precisely that reason. We live in a society so focused on the end game, on getting to the destination, that we even do this with our awakening. We talk about being *awake* or *woke* as if it ends there, when truly, "to awaken" should be used as a verb rather than as a noun or adjective. To awaken is to experience an infinite process of becoming.

In previous decades and centuries, mystics embarked on an intentional and dedicated path toward awakening, and indeed, they still do. A traditional spiritual awakening can be created in many ways including joining a monastic or spiritual tradition, studying with teachers and masters, cloistering oneself in temples and meditation vessels, and delving deeply into a dedicated, guided, and purposeful awakening.

Currently, as I see it in my Reiki and Intuitive Healing practice, individuals are waking up in an entirely different way and at an accelerated rate, primarily through the often shattering experience of crisis and/or transition. This type of awakening was not necessarily chosen on a conscious level, but instead on that of the soul. The individuals embarking on this kind of unexpected awakening often do not realize what they've been through until they are well in the midst of it, floundering and struggling to find resources and support. There are also those who do not fully grasp what has occurred until they are on the other side.

Those who are awakening through crisis may find themselves without teachers and guides to explain this often destabilizing, confusing, and painful process. Conversely, those who embark upon the awakening experience intentionally are often aware of or, at minimum, have some sense of where to turn with questions or for support. Yet many of us are isolated from a spiritual community due to cultural norms, rejection of, or eventual distancing from organized religion. Therefore, we not only find ourselves without guides to whom to turn, but often we reject religious or spiritual support entirely. Learning what to do in this kind of situation, is the premise and goal of this book.

CHAPTER 2

DEFINING THE AWAKENING PROCESS

Each spiritual tradition describes and defines the awakening process in unique ways; however, the underlying experience and end result is almost always the same: to become closer to the divine in the pursuit of greater levels of self and soul-development. One of the most commonly referenced kinds of awakenings in Eastern traditions is the Kundalini awakening in which the serpent's energy that sits at the base of the spine coils itself around the spine and zings up into the crown, prompting physical, mental, and emotional shifts. In Islam, Sufism is the branch that studies mysticism and qualities associated with the awakening experience. Samadhi in Qabalism includes embarking upon the Hermetic path, which may also prompt or create a spiritual awakening. The Yoruba practice Ifa and Orisa Traditions and through the process of divination gain insight and understanding that is used to achieve one's destiny, with destiny including knowledge, wisdom and good character. Because destiny is synonymous with the Will of the Creator, the spiritual path includes continued discovery to achieve a deeper conversation with God.

In Zen Buddhism they speak of Satori (Japanese) or Wu (Chinese) as personal enlightenment, in which the individual sees into his or her true nature. This experience is also called kenshō and offers a delving into the emptiness of the mind. The unexpected type of awakening we explore in this book is called Aparka Mag in Zen Buddhism, in which enlightenment is thrust upon a person, seemingly from out of nowhere.

In Christian traditions, the term *spiritual awakening* is used quite frequently and is most often associated with becoming closer to Christ and God. In pagan, tribal and shamanic traditions pre-dating Christianity (many of which are still practiced today and/or being revived), awakening experiences are undergone in ceremony and ritual.

In contemporary esoteric, mystical, and neo-spiritual communities, the awakening process is also referred to as the Ascension experience, which moves an individual into higher states of consciousness, and is correlated to subtle and extreme shifts and changes in the energy body.

Some religions also have different ways of referring to touching or merging with the divine. Islam speaks of "seeing God's face," and Kundalini is termed "the fire of separation." Christianity speaks of the "incendium amoris," Taoism of the "clumsy fire," and Tibetans of the "tumo heat."

Even for spiritually-organized secular groups, like Alcoholics Anonymous, the awakening process referred to in the *Big Book* occurs when sobriety is accepted, and the person undergoes a complete rebirth as the old alcoholic self is left behind and a new, sober version emerges.

An awakening is, at its heart, a rebirth process marked by profound and deep transformation. An awakening can start with something miniscule and snowball into a massive shift in which everything is questioned and next to nothing stays the same.

Key Elements of an Awakening

A quick internet search will turn up dozens of articles dedicated to describing the signs and symptoms of a modern-day spiritual awakening. While most are based on anecdotal experiences, and some have greater veracity than others, most of the literature (both academic and anecdotal) reveal recurrent themes and categories that describe an awakening. It may be helpful also to think of the transformative nature of an awakening experience in which one version of a person is metaphorically dying to be replaced by a completely new version. This type of death usually requires chaos which exists everywhere in nature as the inherent catalyst of change. As an awakening experience is at its very core a transformative event, chaos theory can help us understand the underpinnings of an awakening.

In his book *Human Tuning*, Dr. John Beaulieu explores sound healing from a scientific perspective, and uses chaos theory to describe the sound healing process[5]. He defines energy fields as two or more points in space that are connected by a medium, and this connection is expressed as a tone or vibration. In his description, he references Dr. Hans Jenny's work[6] with cymatics to provide an understanding of energy fields and their dynamics. Dr. Jenny used metal plates with substances like sand, fluid, and powder placed atop them to observe how vibration affects these substances. Specifically, Dr. Jenny observed the patterns created by the substances based on different vibrational frequencies.

Two factors are of particular importance to our understanding of transformation and the awakening process: the first is the concept of nodes. In these cymatics experiments, nodes are the areas on the vibrating plate that do not move. In systems science, these nodes are called attractors because this area of non-movement draws everything toward it. These nodes, or attractors, are what allow one energy field to shift or change into another. In the healing arts, we call these nodes still point. Other terms we use to describe this phase of transformation are neutral, liminal stage, interstitial, and even "the calm before the storm."

In our healing work, still point is purposefully induced to help make the transition from one state of being into another more easeful. In hypnosis, this is done through trance. In my Reiki practice, I create this with meditation and aromatherapy. In our own personal work, we may do this with meditation, journaling, or creating time and space for reflection. Rest and quieting of the mind is crucial to inducing still point.

The second key component Dr. Beaulieu introduces is the concept of chaos, which immediately ensues after still point as the old energy field is drawn toward the node or attractor. The old field must disorganize itself before a new field can emerge.

Dr. Ilya Prigogine researched chaos theory in terms of thermodynamic systems. He found that all living beings emit more and more energy over time, causing dissonances in the system. Much like the vibrating metal plate, the increase in this energy emission increases the dissonance causing the system to wobble more and more over time until chaos ensues and everything disorganizes in order to reorganize itself again.

Using the concepts of still point and chaos, we can look back on major changes in our life to see where the first whispers of that *wobbling* began. This beginning can usually be traced from minor events that coalesced into one large event that we may perceive as a crisis. It's from this crisis that has produced chaos that a new system, energy structure, or way of being can be introduced.

Dr. Beaulieu offers that, in an ideal world, when we anticipate a new pattern arising in our lives, we would move into still point and allow the new pattern to emerge[7]. Through this anticipation and movement, we would find the experience of chaos less debilitating. While likely still uncomfortable to some extent, we wouldn't experience the massive crises that many of us create around transitions in our lives, primarily because we fight chaos rather than moving into neutrality and allowing it to occur.

In spiritual paradigms, we talk a great deal about surrender and non-attachment, being present, integrating, and even returning to nature. In many ways, these are all concepts that support the function of still point, as is accepting chaos as a natural and vital part of life and transformation. In tribal cultures and shamanic traditions, chaos energy is revered and celebrated. It is invited into ceremony as a key component to rites of passage, shamanic initiations, and cultural traditions. Interestingly, chaos is also associated with the feminine element which has been historically marginalized and stigmatized, along with aspects associated with feminine "messiness," "over emotionality," and "unpredictability."

Our Western society values order and achievement above almost anything else. It's no wonder that a crisis is often what is needed to produce change as we have no space in our lives to induce still point: to rest and allow ourselves to simply *be*. We find that we must break free of the need for constant doing and achieving so we can create enough space for a new version of ourselves to emerge.

I believe this is, in part, why the awakening experience can be so painful. I've often found that the stronger and more active/thinking/rigid a person is, the much more challenging their awakening process can be. These are the individuals I see fighting against the chaos, seeking to understand the process from a cerebral perspective, looking for the science behind each step of growth, and butting their head against new ways of being by trying to solve a challenge with the same thinking and behaviors that created it. Often, this approach also can express itself as avoidance behavior, in which we continually ignore the signs trying to point us toward change. Sometimes this occurs through numbing agents like drug-use, alcohol, pornography and/or relationship addiction. Indeed, I've found some of our most sensitive individuals, those who are most primed for an awakening, seek ways to desensitize themselves to life, because they haven't been given the skills to navigate what they are feeling and experiencing.

At some point, the System of You will seek to change. A major change of this System of You is what I would posit is one way to view the awakening experience. Within this context, the types of events or experiences that may describe an awakening experience include[8]:

- A sense of loneliness and not belonging inside of one's life any longer.

- Questioning everything, and feelings of uncertainty about life; this may include feelings of confusion, stagnation and also an inability to make definitive choices.

- Physical symptoms of pain that may not have any identifiable physical origination.

- Health crises that do have physical origination and are often exacerbated by stress and unhealthy behaviors that the awakening process is specifically attempting to address.

- Surges of emotion from panic and anxiety, to depression and crying incessantly, to euphoria and bliss (often experienced drastically, leaping from one set of emotions to another).

- Loss of passion, a longing to go "home," and/or feelings of neutrality and lack of enthusiasm about life.

- Withdrawal from relationships including family, friends, community, and work. This could include only certain relationships, or be a complete withdrawal, including introversion or isolation. Often, the relationships that are most intimate are those that are withdrawn from, precisely because of the need for distance in order to change.

- Sudden drastic shifts in key components of one's life including quitting one's job, breaking up with a romantic partner, packing up and moving, changing diet and exercise habits, etc.

- Difficulty in describing the experience to friends and family, either in fear that they will not understand, and/or because the individual doesn't yet understand it. Often there is a sense that words are lacking to accurately describe the experience.

- Intense dreaming, headaches, altered states of perception, sleeplessness, and restlessness.

- A sense of connection to something that is greater than oneself, and perhaps anything that may have been experienced previously. This often presents itself as an epiphany, the breaking of the metaphoric *crisis fever* in which there is a feeling of having gained access to wisdom and emotions that are sacred, special, and so immense that words cannot describe it.

While not everyone's awakening includes all of these experiences, and/or individuals may undergo other symptoms, these comprise the most frequent occurrences associated with the awakening process. It's important to note that these all eventually pass, and that working with spiritual leaders as well as professionals in psychology and/or the healing arts, can assist in moving through the most challenging components.

CHAPTER 3

WHO, WHEN & HOW?

To Whom Do Awakenings Happen?

One of the simultaneously beautiful and terrifying parts of the unexpected awakening process is that it can happen to anybody: any walk of life, any age, any income level and (even while the old spiritual paradigm would question this) any level of spiritual belief or non-belief.

I have seen atheists awaken just as fully and completely as those holding deep spiritual and philosophical commitments. I sometimes feel those who are the least prepared for it, perhaps even the least willing at first, can have the deepest transformations. This is because they must journey through such a vast and wide array of new and very different experiences to get to the new version of themselves. The leap from the old self to the new self is that much more pronounced and steep for those people, especially when the previous version of self had rejected all things related to growth, the unknown, and anything which science cannot readily prove or explain.

I've also found Who to be a less relevant question than When. I believe that if anything influences an awakening at its deepest and most profound level, it's timing.

When Do Awakenings Occur?

I often think the awakening process, much as it's described in Kundalini practices, sits dormant until the perfect combination of people, places, and events intersect. As described above, in addition to the awakening experience propelling itself into our lives, each individual always has the opportunity to engage with it as deeply as he or she would like, including not engaging with it at all. How many times have you been on the precipice of something enormous - a shift in a pattern or behavior you absolutely knew was for the best - and yet walked away from it and continued on with old ways of being and doing?

Awakenings, in many cases, are a culmination of all those moments when we walked away. Over time, those moments moved from that famous whisper to a shout to a scream. When we refuse to listen to the signs that point toward better opportunities for happiness and growth, those signs get bigger and bigger until we find ourselves inside of a full-blown crisis with the potential to become an unexpected awakening.

In preparation for the writing of this book, I asked each contributor to create a personal timeline of key events in their lives, starting from as early as they could remember. I asked them to spend several days to weeks on it, adding to it as moments spontaneously came to mind. From there, they spent time highlighting the events they felt were particularly profound in their process of becoming a new, and "better" version of themselves. This process alone was illuminating for all of us, myself included, as we realized that we had experienced many awakenings over the course of our lifetimes. We also realized that the experience we had most immediately and readily defined as our spiritual awakening was actually predicated much earlier than we'd originally thought.

As we journeyed together through the process, each contributor could see more clearly a perfectly traceable trajectory of personal development, albeit a winding and tumultuous one. For many, myself included, those earliest whispers that each of us avoided hearing and acting upon were ignored quite purposefully primarily because we simply weren't ready for any other course at the time. This hindsight can be incredibly valuable when we remove the shame, blame, or guilt that comes from judgment statements like: "Well, I should have figured that out sooner," and instead replace judgment with acceptance statements, such as: "What an amazing trajectory my growth has taken. Why, perhaps, was I unready to awaken, or transform, earlier in my life?" Similar helpful questions include: "What did I learn from those moments when I walked away from a different way of being? What did I learn from the choices I made instead?" You'll see many of these very questions posed and answered in the stories in this collection.

Key types of experiences that can propel an unexpected awakening often look like a crisis and are almost always tied to key transitional moments in life. That is because the awakening process quite adeptly looks for the perfect time, the perfect opportunity to shake everything up. What better time than when we are already embarking upon some kind of change?

Sometimes these awakening experiences, however, are propelled upon us in violent ways that have nothing to do with our own personal responsibility or contribution to the event. These types of experiences include natural disasters, abuse or assault, the unexpected death of a loved one, to name just a few. These types of experiences are also included in this work, as the contributors have so bravely sought to share how they created a spiritual awakening out of the dregs of some of the most brutal and challenging moments any of us might undergo.

Based on my own personal and professional observations, I've loosely categorized the types of experiences in which I most often see an awakening occur. These include, but most certainly are not limited to:

- abuse, assault, rape, or the experience of violent/traumatic acts
- addiction of all kinds (alcohol, substance, relationship, eating, etc.)
- breakups (romantic relationship, divorce)
- changes in family, friendship, or community structure and dynamics
- changes in identity (coming out, gender identity)
- geographic move/travel
- job/career change
- life-or-death experiences (near death experience, death of a loved one, suicide attempt)
- natural disasters, community crises
- new relationship(s)/community
- physical and/or emotional/mental health obstacles and/or illness
- pursuing a new spiritual or educational path, or the completion thereof

Many individuals undergoing an awakening may find themselves in the midst of multiple transition points, occurring all at once. It's not uncommon for me to work with a client who is simultaneously in the midst of a break up, has lost his/her job, and is experiencing a health crisis while moving homes. Alternately, individuals may experience a domino effect, in which one area shifts, which leads to change in another area, and so on in a more gradual trajectory. Either way, the purpose of the awakening experience is to bring us into greater alignment with our true self and our soul's purpose. As such, if we have numerous areas in our lives that have become out of alignment with bringing us joy and purpose, the awakening process will seek out those places to induce shift.

How Do Awakenings Occur?

We become like the Phoenix rising from the ashes, and yet often, it doesn't look nearly as romantic, poetic, or glorious as what that mythic image invokes. Perhaps a better image is of clawing up and out of a pit of horrific-smelling muck, naked in the midst of torrential acid rain.

This isn't to say that everyone who has an unexpected awakening experiences it in a painful way. I have met a handful of people who, through some incredible process of what I'll call karmic-gifting, have been able to come out the other side of an awakening relatively unscathed. As we've discussed before, the very nature of the awakening process usually requires some kind of chaos and transformation, which, let's be honest, most of us don't make the space for, much less embrace in a loving gentle way. Most of us are awakening unexpectedly precisely because so few of us are choosing another way.

We live in a mostly masculine-dominated society, where our every action is guided by the principles of go, do, achieve, act, create, push through, and don't stop. How challenging and painful the awakening experience becomes is directly correlated to how intent we are on pushing through at Mach speed, controlling, endlessly *doing*, and not stopping to integrate. Awakenings happen best, or I should say, with as little pain as possible, when we surrender. How many of us even know how to do that, let alone value it as a key part of life? So that a new version of who we are can emerge, the awakening process requires a lot of *not doing*, a lot of being with the feminine element of receiving, opening, and allowing, as well as dancing with chaos, mystery, the unknown, and the creative self.

I believe unexpected awakenings happen during times of transition or immense crisis because those are precisely the moments when we are most willing to let go of old ways of being and try something new.

CHAPTER 4

STAGES OF AN UNEXPECTED AWAKENING

Articles site anywhere from three to twelve stages of an awakening. While stages are less important than is the experience itself, having a framework can provide a helpful overview of the process, as well as an understanding of where one currently stands in their awakening. And so, in an effort to support those going through an unexpected awakening, here is my offering to the stages as I've experienced them myself, and have seen them experienced by others:

1. Crisis
2. Intervention/Reorganization
3. Liminal Stage/Still Point
4. Rebirth/Joy
5. Perpetual Becoming

For those of us not on the dedicated mystic's path (perhaps even for those who are), the goal may not necessarily be to merge or find unity with the divine. For many of us dedicated to having a deeply human experience as a jumping off point for spiritual transformation and growth, our spiritual development necessarily takes place on the stage of life. While I don't expect everyone reading this book to agree with me, for better or worse we came here to Earth to experience our humanness. In the pursuit of higher spiritual truths, we often actually find ourselves shirking off our humanity with the goal of running away from that which is painful in the human experience, rather than breathing into it and allowing the experience to grow us.

I'm not saying that this is easy: there's a reason why this is called the warrior's journey or the hero's path. When we are truly committed, we realize we are always becoming, always returning to the beginner's path, riding the great cyclical wave of perpetual becoming.

Stage One: Crisis

While the issues that have fueled an awakening have been occurring long before the point of crisis, this is usually the most distinguishable moment of the awakening process. The point of crisis is the time during which we begin to question what is happening to us, and why. This very questioning is the light bulb that goes off illuminating that something in life needs to change. It is the seed of this change, the idea fueling a need to *do things differently* that signals the awakening process to begin. This is akin to the wobbly metal plate moving the system into chaos.

Very few people stop here but we can probably all think of at least one person we know who has. This would be someone we think of as existing in perpetual crisis mode or someone who constantly appears to be a victim. On the surface they look as though they are trying to tend to the crisis, while usually they are overly reliant on the support and aide of others. Typically, someone who becomes stuck in Stage One exhausts resource after resource, often burning one bridge of support, just to move on to the next. With professional support, it's possible for these people to move on to the next stage, although this is often very difficult.

Stage Two: Intervention/Reorganization

Once the crisis ensues, typically we do what all human beings do: we try to fix it. Usually this looks like quite a bit of floundering as, at first, we turn to the tools and coping skills we learned or picked up along the way in life. Rarely, though, can we use the same tools or thinking to solve the crisis that created it in the first place. It is at this intervention stage that many people find they are unwilling to create true shift, and so they patch the crisis up the best way they can with the tools they have on hand, until an even larger crisis emerges. This patching up pattern continues until the system either shifts, or eventually becomes so rigid and stuck that a person becomes bitter and unhappy and, in the most extreme cases, sick and even dying.

If, however, the individual commits to a process of change and transformation while inside of this intervention stage, they will begin to seek out new tools, new coping skills, and new methods with which to fix their crisis. As new skills and tools come on board, small shifts begin to occur, and the new pattern begins to be introduced. This can feel like a false sense of true awakening because the process has only just begun, but pain has usually started to subside, and there is a sense that there is a way forward. There are tools and movement toward a new way of life. Each of these small victories toward fixing the initial crisis feel like big wins.

This is another stage in which a person can also pause or remain indefinitely. Perhaps the crisis, on a surface level, has been abated with new ways of thinking and being. If there isn't a commitment to a deeper path of self-growth, often individuals will go back to their lives as they were, quite happy with their new skill set until crisis hits again.

As I work with individuals on their timelines of healing, I see this pattern occurring frequently, and have seen it also for myself. It is one of the most common ways that we grow and learn. We come up against a problem, we attempt to solve it, the old ways no longer work, we find new ways, we solve it, and we're done. We move on with life. While this is certainly important and vital to our growth and development, it does not an awakening make.

Stage Three: Liminal / Still Point

Time and again, I've seen that a true awakening is actually created in this liminal stage. It is in the interstitial place, the neutral place of still point, where true awakenings occur. When we slow down enough to allow a new pattern to overtake our lives, we realize that something incredible has happened, and we no longer want to dive back into our old lives. We not only want the fix to the crisis with a moderate improvement to our lives; instead we want a whole new way of living and being in the world. We want an entirely new version of self.

One of the challenges in this stage is to sit in it. This is the awkward, quiet, unmoving stage of winter. Everything has died, some new pieces have emerged on the surface, but the true and real rebirth is being called into those nodes or attractors. Just as we must journey through winter and into spring, we must sit in this place of surrender doing very little other than practicing patience as we integrate what often feels like too much to bear. Relationships often end in this stage, even those we hadn't purposefully sought to sever. Like a field suddenly going fallow, everything around us seems to die and transition, as the awakening process takes on a life of its own. We no longer recognize ourselves or our lives, and we don't yet have a firm grip on what is emerging.

You can see why most people turn back here. This place of endings and waiting is often categorized by a feeling of being cheated, of having done something wrong, and the need to *do* or *learn* or *create* more because we find so much discomfort in silence and waiting. We are a very impatient society.

This is where the commitment to personal growth becomes so important. Those who are committed to a new way journey through this interstitial place, often kicking and screaming, but journey through it they do. They learn to meditate. They take up yoga. They find creative pursuits. They sit in nature. They allow themselves to get lost and flounder. They learn the beauty of the term Elizabeth Gilbert references in *Eat, Pray, Love*: dolce far niente - the sweetness of doing nothing.

Once we have surrendered, we may not even be aware of the seeds that are finally beginning to plant themselves at the end of winter as we move into spring. These seeds are beginning to grow ever so slowly under our surface. This quiet place also allows us to feel their germination, to hear and experience the quiet beating heart of that which has not quite yet been born.

Stage Four: Rebirth & Joy

The rebirth that occurs after the liminal stage contains a different kind of joy than that which is achieved after the intervention stage. It is not the joy of fixing a problem, it is the euphoria of seeing oneself emerge from a chrysalis as a completely new person. This is the joy I watch happen with clients, usually several years (yes, *years*) after the initial crisis that prompted the unexpected awakening. It is the moment, after so much hard work, that there is a sense that life is truly different: not just on a surface level, not just in the *facts* of one's life. This joy comes from a place of feeling, from the inner core that I'd call the soul level. The soul has been lifted up and out of the old systems and patterns that kept it caged, small, and unhealthy. The subsequent emergence spans such great depths that it feels like an orgasmic stretch after a long period of hibernation.

This is another place where many stop in their awakening. It is less a *turning back* (although old systems can certainly return), but more a resting place. We may choose to sit in the light of this euphoria for many more years. We may also choose to allow our egos to get the better of us during this stage, causing old systems to return and we find ourselves back in Stage One.

Stage Five: Perpetual Becoming

At some point after rebirth, most who have gone through an awakening will eventually pick up the walking stick again and choose to carry on, purposefully and with a sense of dedicated commitment toward the next step in personal development and growth. If we are intentional with our process, we are usually (but not always) able to prevent another crisis of drastic proportions. Even if we cannot prevent it, we see crisis differently: less as a disaster and more as a red flag, pointing us to the next place of growth along our path.

That said, none of us have the answers to all the mysteries of the universe, or the answers to why events happen as they do. We'll never know exactly why bad things happen to good people. I think about 90 percent of the time we can trace the origin of a crisis to a behavior, choice, or pattern. The remaining 10 percent of the time, we cannot account for why someone is raped, murdered, assaulted, hit by a car, or loses a loved one, etc. After a phase of grief, pain, and being with the experience, however, we can always understand how we can create a blessing and growth out of what appears to be a curse. Many of us also accept that these crisis points were on some level orchestrated by the soul for our highest and deeper learning and growth.

Either way, this final stage is actually not final at all. In my opinion and experience, it is another beginning. Often, the lessons and experiences get harder and more challenging as we continue to make our way up the mountain. Underhill calls this the true dark night of the soul. Dr. Walters describes it as,

> after bliss, after the many convolutions and returns, there is, suddenly, a seeming withdrawal of divine favor. Bliss, which may have become a regular feature of one's life, suddenly departs and one is left to ponder what has gone wrong...according to Underhill this grief is greater than any experienced earlier, because we have now 'tasted God,' known the divine splendor of acceptance...we discover (again) that the journey is not under our control, that it is directed by some still-mysterious force seemingly both within and outside of the self. We must release all attempts to guide a force or return to the earlier state, and simply stand still and wait in patience and humility for the renewal of connection...And as the process continues our energies become ever more delicate, ever more refined. What once arrived as a great storm of thunder and lightning now comes quietly, resembling soft rain falling on the trees in the forest.[9]

By the time we've found ourselves in Stage Five, most have learned the beauty of our humanness. Our spiritual path begins to happen on the human level in an entirely new way. Spirituality is not seen as a separate act, but is interwoven into every moment of life. The euphoria we felt in Stages Two and Four is rarely found in the same pronounced capacity as before. And after a period of time, we stop trying to search for that high, and instead find the quiet, deep beauty contained within life's juxtaposed joys and sorrows.

Having outlined these stages, I'd like to add a caution that these stages cannot be forced. You may identify the particular stage (or stages) you find yourself in, but rather than looking to hurry up and complete it -- trying to get to the finish line -- I'd instead invite you to journey more deeply *into* the stage you're in. Learn everything you can about the process, soak it in and reap as much growth as you can. The ability to *be* in the moment, unattached and exactly where you are, is the only act that will allow you to complete the stage and move onto the next. Awakening is so much more about learning to be, and much less about accomplishing and doing.

CHAPTER 5

AWAKENINGS & EGO

I find ego gets a bad rap in modern-day spirituality. It is most often associated with only one side of the ego coin: the shadow side. Ego, in its shadow expression, embodies pride, attachment, arrogance, rigidity, and selfishness. Qualities which, indeed, we are best served by moving past.

Yet ego also provides us with a vital and necessary function through which we are able to engage and interact with the external world: identity. Psychoanalyst Carl Jung defined the ego as the center of the field of consciousness[10]. From a psychological perspective, Jung's concept of a person in its completeness is called the *self*. The self is comprised of various components with the ego being just one, and yet a necessary one. The ego's primary purpose centers around identity and the overtly intellectual processes of the mind. In essence, the ego is a command center of sorts that selects the information that is relevant from a person's internal world to engage with the outer world in that particular moment in time[11].

Without ego, we would be left wandering around uncertain of who we are, where we are going, and how we can best engage with ourselves and our relationships. If we look at identity from a Jungian perspective, when the ego is operating in harmony with a deeper understanding of the other darker and perhaps less healed parts of the psyche (such as the shadow, inner child, and personas/complexes), we are better able to fully express the self. This means we have a strong sense of who we are at all levels of the psyche, as well as the soul, allowing us to be capable and even exultant in the shifting of that expression in our human experience.

The questioning and even temporary destruction of the old ego or identity, but not its complete eradication, is a key component of the awakening experience. An awakening occurs as one version of the self is necessarily questioned, then surrenders and crumbles, so that a new version can emerge. Hopefully, this version of the self has a healthier relationship to all sides of the ego - both bright and shadow sides because, as shadow theory tells us, we all have shadow. Shadow is a necessary part of our experience as the light cannot exist without the dark. Ego will always necessarily embody both components. Our continued work post- and perpetual-awakening is to be aware of the way in which we must dance with our shadow lest it grow in the dark regions of the self to which we banish it.

This leads to the other place where I often see ego arising in the awakening process. It can even come in the simple definition of being *awakened*. When we overly attach to ourselves as being *spiritual*, having *awakened* or being *woke*, the shadow side of ego can rear its ugly head yet again, and we begin to lord over others this new power, awareness, or wisdom we feel we've gained.

We've seen it time and again in Western spiritual communities in which the term *guru* has been self-appropriated by individuals who don't understand its core meaning, removed as it is from its originating cultural context. Riding high on this power, certain spiritual leaders become spiritual abusers, and tyrants in extreme cases. When they hold their higher spiritual status above that of their disciples, we see events like mass ritual suicide and cults.

It's an understandable progression, as I think of my own awakening experience. Most of us feel, on the other side of the dark night of the soul, that we have hit the metaphoric spiritual summit. After a period of intense suffering, we not only feel better, but often we are overcome with glee and euphoria. We want to share this experience with everyone we know, and we may feel we are uniquely capable of becoming a healer, an advisor, an author, a life coach, a guru.

This euphoric stage is incredible and understandable, as hard won as it was. The answers to everything appear to be so simple, and we begin to apply whatever new metaphysical or spiritual lingo we learned from online courses, blogs, classes or indeed, books such as this. Because there is little requirement for any kind of professional certification of the awakening process (not that I am promoting any such idea), we find ourselves inside of a society rampant with self-help, personal growth, and spiritual development "leaders," people who themselves are still attempting to figure life out.

I'll be the first to claim that I am one of these individuals. Even though I was first exposed to these ideas at an early age (my parents began studying metaphysics and hypnotherapy when I was in my early teens), I am relatively new to the community of individuals who practice the healing arts. Those who knew me before my most profound awakening many years ago may very well laugh at the idea of taking life or spiritual advice from me.

This is where our work with ego comes to the forefront. It is in owning and recognizing that we must keep an eye to ego. And in this way, we continue to grow and learn. We continue to embrace our shadow. We continue to find the humility that comes from admitting all that we don't understand. We are careful of thinking we know the answer to anyone else's questions or path. We commit to being perpetual students. Many of the most awakened individuals I know, are much more focused on listening, than on talking.

Inside of this newly empowered place, we may also feel called to buy t-shirts with spiritual slogans, post memes that appear trendy, and even appropriate other culture's spiritual traditions (see Chapter 6). However, the materialization and commodification of spirituality is a slippery slope – both because it can reinforce the shadow side of ego if left unchecked, and can also do damage to other cultures if we misappropriate and dilute their sacred spiritual traditions. It's also important that we not confuse this outward expression of ego and identity with the inward work that has only barely begun on the other side of awakening.

Being lulled into a false sense of achievement and status can cause us to fall back into the ego trap our awakening has attempted to pull us away from. Additionally, the moment when we are jubilantly celebrating, is usually also the point just before it becomes much, much more challenging. After an awakening, we have only just arrived at one summit of many. The further we delve into our issues, the more we commit to our spiritual work, the harder and more challenging the lessons become. We can again make the error of attaching a value judgment to this - that the harder our life becomes the more spiritual we are.

The most incredibly spiritual people I have met, are exactly that: people. They have traversed through some of the most heinous challenges life has had to offer and have come out the other side somehow still capable of loving others and seeing the world as a place of opportunity and possibility, rather than as a place of pain, misery, and hatred.

I also feel the term *humility* gets a bad rap, in part because we associate it with shame or guilt, of crouching down, staying small, minimizing our gifts so as to not take up too much space. Yet humility, as I see it, is a beautiful antidote to the shadow side of the ego. Humility is actually an owning of all that we have experienced, of our challenges and areas of growth, and recognizing decisions we might have made differently. Humility is the place we say, "Yes, I have learned so much, and yet, oh my goodness, there is so much more left to learn."

Humility is also where we learn to listen to others, especially to those who we believe may not even merit our ear. From here, we see everyone as a teacher, and we allow ourselves to move into the seat of student. This is the heart of the beginner's path, of perpetual becoming. We agree to begin again in each moment, from the now, being fully present to what is unfolding in front of us, and unattached to the outcome.

CHAPTER 6

PRIVILEGE

During the awakening process, and even throughout the spiritual journey, individuals sometimes feel the desire to take from other cultures' traditions, a term we call cultural appropriation or misappropriation. From a sociological perspective, consensual sharing of cultural traditions is part of the evolutionary process, and how most of us arrived at whatever cultural mixture comprises our unique heritage[12]. Additionally, we may choose to follow a specific religious or spiritual path, or learn healing arts traditions, that do not come from our own heritage, but have been made globally and consensually available to all people, regardless of ethnicity.

However, cultural appropriation can become harmful when the culture doing the taking is dominant, and the culture being taken from is not, and especially when the taking is not consensual, and/or is removed from the originating context. Ultimately this can lead to the loss of the originating culture's belief or practice, as it is corrupted in favor of the dominant culture's version, with the originating culture's practices being diluted or abandoned. When we are considering what we may adopt in our spiritual practice that comes from another culture, three main guidelines to consider are consent, power dynamics and preservation/respect of cultural traditions.

Frequently in current metaphysical and new age movements, we culturally appropriate without thought to these three issues. These types of misappropriation typically include objects, language, practices, ceremonies, symbols, clothing, adornment and traditions, and are typically taken piecemeal. By taking it out of the culture and context in which it is meant to be used, we do damage both to the power and sacredness that is held by the originating culture, and we add to the long legacy of colonization.

I find this occurs, in large part, because many white Westerners in particular have lost a sense of connection to spirituality and are searching for non-Christian perspectives on religion and spirituality. For reasons more elaborate than this book has space to explore, many individuals have rejected organized Western religion and look toward other cultures' religions and philosophies. However, our privileged viewpoint makes us blind to thinking twice before purchasing products or utilizing language we like, in an effort to feel or look more spiritual, without thinking of the impact our actions and words have.

Many individuals on a spiritual path feel an undercurrent sense that tribal and shamanic cultures somehow seem closer to Source, and indeed they often are. This is in large part because these traditions have been preserved quite carefully and through great duress over hundreds and even thousands of years. Many individuals who feel disconnected from their own ethnic spiritual roots become fascinated with indigenous cultures in an effort to find this same closeness, this same sacredness, believing that the answer lies there rather than within.

While we certainly have much to learn from indigenous and tribal communities and cultures, we can do great damage by walking into these worlds without a sense of respect and reverence for their lives and lands, and especially taking and using whatever we like. Often we are blind to the Western world's propensity to take what it wants without asking, as well as attempting to wear (often quite literally) others' spiritual traditions.

In my personal spiritual journey, I've been drawn to a wide variety of spiritual practices. I've traveled across the world as part of my seeking, and eventually have settled in New Mexico, partly due to its deep and rich culture of First Nations People tribes and communities. And I've seen first-hand how cultural appropriation negatively impacts the originating culture. Colonization is occurring now on a spiritual level; this further damages communities that have fought hard to preserve their identities and traditions, struggling not to be whitewashed or have their very powerful language and practices reduced down to a meme, or a slogan on a t-shirt.

For those of us who can trace our heritage back to European cultural traditions that pre-date Christianity, we are learning more about the pagan and neo-pagan traditions that are ardently being revived. Once we shuck off the negative connotation created during the conquest of native European tribal cultures by the Christians, we understand that paganism at its heart is simply an honoring of earth-based spiritual traditions. Tracing our own ancestry can provide another route for those of us seeking this type of deeper tribal experience; herein we may find a connection to pre-Christian spiritual traditions that may give the same feeling of sacred closeness to Source.

I've been grateful to be invited to participate and witness indigenous and tribal ceremonies and practices of many different kinds, but I do not put my experience on display. I don't speak about what I've privately seen or been invited to, and spiritual gifts or tokens that have been gifted to me, I now keep in private. When I attend the public ceremonies that indigenous communities quite generously invite the public to witness, I hold space, witness from a place of respect, and also ensure that those around me are doing the same, even if that means educating a stranger on the spot.

Another component of our privilege that bears mentioning, lies in the spiritual narrative that is being created, where we also whitewash conversations, social media platforms and classes, effectively erasing or negating the voices of Black, Indigenous and People of Color (BIPOC). We negate their experiences, and often do not invite BIPOC to be at the table for dialogue and conversation, or if we do, often it is only a token offering. We create classes without taking BIPOC into account, and we don't fully consider how the language we use may reinforce cultural stereotypes and/or power dynamics. You can visit UnexpectedAwakenings.com for a list of authors, teachers and social media accounts you may consider following regarding this topic.

Finally, I also find the awakening process itself, as the Western World currently experiences it, to be one of privilege. In the sense that for many to make meaning of their experience as a spiritual awakening (versus the act of simply surviving) means time, space, and a certain amount of security to engage with crisis in this way, and perhaps more importantly, to want to tout it as an awakening in the first place.

CHAPTER 7

WHY DO WE AWAKEN?

I leave Why for last because it's a question that may provide some interesting explorations, yet all too often we ruminate over asking "Why?" when the answer is either inconsequential, or incredibly simple. In the awakening experience there is beauty in the simplicity of the answer to why we awaken:

Growth.

Everything in nature seeks to evolve, to grow, to change, to become a better version of that which it had previously been. I believe this growth is an enormous part of why so many of us are unexpectedly awakening, all at once, during these intense and transformative times. If we are to survive as a planet, as a species, as a global community intent on something, anything, other than greed and wealth, we must grow personally and then we must grow collectively.

You can choose to see an awakening as spiritual, or not. The more important question is, are you becoming a better version of yourself? And yes, *better* is subjective and self-determined.

There are myriad other answers to the question Why, which are likely deeply personal and unique to you.

We focus so much on Why as a society: it's a question we could go round and round with infinitely, without ever arriving at a definitive answer. I personally find How to be a much more productive question, as it illuminates the trajectory of our growth. And when we ask How and Why together, we arrive at the most complete answer: Why provides us with an anchor point as to the purpose of our awakening, and How shows us each twist and turn, as well as the tools and skills we developed along the way.

All these ponderings aside, as you awaken more fully you'll likely come to understand that You are always the most important reason Why.

PART 2: STORIES OF UNEXPECTED AWAKENINGS

CHAPTER 8

GRACE

Juliet Erickson

All of my immediate family members are dead. I'm older now than my siblings will ever be but young enough that my parents never lived to see my first wrinkle.

It's not the fact that all of them are dead that makes me want to share this story. Rather, because of their relatively abrupt disappearance from my life that has left me with an unexpected earthy, bittersweet clarity that I can only describe as a refined sense of trust in, and kindness for, myself. I learned that even in the face of darkest adversity and loss, my most reliable first step has always been in trusting that I would get through it.

The death of my family members did not happen all at once. Not one tragic event, but over a relatively short time, it was one after the other.

My brother was first to go. He was in a car accident, but he didn't die immediately. His injuries resulted in quadriplegia and, after eight weeks in neurological intensive care, he suffocated and died from pneumonia. It seemed to happen so fast. Every day his recovery faltered. It was difficult to leave the hospital. Nights and days of little to no sleeping in the waiting rooms, strangers distraught as a result of their own bad news down the hall, bad light and air and even worse food, visits from well-meaning but unwelcome acquaintances. The day before he died he did his best to hug me. Lying there with his head pierced in traction tongs, barely able to breathe, he smiled and signaled for me to crawl underneath his arm.

Anyone who has lost a child or a sibling knows the relentless and unforgiving toll it can take on the lives of those left behind. This tragedy didn't bring our family together. Instead, we coped in isolation and retreated to lick our wounds in separate corners.

I felt somehow that I could or should try and absorb the blow to my parents, so I quit my job, deferred my university term and moved cities to live nearer to my mother until her life got back to a relative equilibrium.

Eventually I realized there was nothing my presence could ever do to soothe the empty space created by my brother's death. I also grew to understand and accept it.

My physical memories of him are represented by a few trinkets collected in a small box in the corner of a single drawer. These include a few photographs of us together as children, a pocket watch, a high school class ring and his Coast Guard marksmanship medal. I occasionally get a passing glance at him looking back at me in a mirror through the similar shape of our nose and curve of an eyebrow. I also remain unbeaten at thumb-wrestling due to my honed skills from our endless matches during lazy summer days.

Shortly after my brother's death I was introduced to the practice of meditation by a friend. At first, the suggestion seemed both amusing and terrifying. Me? Sitting quietly? For HOW long? My friend sensed that I was struggling with an emotional tug-of-war. I kept myself overly distracted and exhausted with work and general busy-ness and was a little afraid of being alone with myself and my thoughts. On the other side of silence, I imagined an overwhelming pull toward a downward spiral of great sadness.

My family wouldn't talk about my brother's death. I couldn't talk about it. We just got on with life.

At first, practicing meditation was difficult. After a few months, I started to appreciate that I was benefiting from this gentle, more structured way to balance the demands I put on myself and making time and space to re-energize and rest. I became more curious and comfortable with the idea of actively cultivating a quieter mind. By this time, I had also become involved as a partner in a business that required regular international travel and a schedule that facilitated fast-paced growth. I was working long hours and placing heavy demands on my physical and emotional health.

Like most of us, the noise and distraction inside our own mind can be an obstacle to meditation and to fully relaxing or nurturing ourselves. Combine our human tendency to seek distraction from painful memories and self-doubt, and it can seem hard to know how to even start to be alone with our thoughts!

I learnt different meditation approaches through reading, studying and practice and settled into a groove that suited me. It was simple, a little irregular, and sacred. I started sitting for only few minutes at a time and built up over time to as many minutes as I needed. I would practice meditating on long plane flights, before tense meetings, as a passenger in a taxi or whenever I found moments that I could be quiet, close my eyes, and focus on my breath. I found that making even a little bit of time and space to meditate was getting easier, and the feeling afterward of being refreshed and invigorated was improving greatly.

Later the following year, my father called me at my home in London one morning and told me he wasn't feeling well. He was just diagnosed with late stage lung cancer and probably wouldn't live more than a week. After his call, I got on the next plane to California and, twenty hours later, I was in his room in a small rural hospital.

Sitting with my father at his bedside, my mind was racing. How odd it must be for him to have been presented with his time of death with such certainty. I sat and looked around the dimly-lit room and noticed how thin he looked under the crisp white sheet. His man-foot sticking out from under the blanket, his very blue eyes, the uneaten container of hospital green Jell-O and the mustard-colored plastic water cup on the tray next to the bed. His flannel shirt and blue-jeans folded on the chair in the corner, his worn-out sneakers untied on the floor. A cheap novel one of the nurses had been reading was left on the sink. In my exhausted jet-lagged-brain fog, I couldn't feel or think clearly.

I smiled sadly to myself as I thought about how often an extraordinary life boils down to the ordinary and essential.

My sister couldn't afford the cost of travel, so I arranged a ticket for her to fly from her home in Hawaii to be here with us. She was particularly close to my father and I could see she was not coping well with the situation. When she arrived she was intoxicated, medicated and wobbly on her feet. Her eyes were puffy from crying and she was pale. The nurses encouraged her to go to the hotel and rest for a while.

My father's decision was to die without the last-ditch effort of chemotherapy. Between morphine injections, he and I discussed his final wishes and some small administrative details that would help me navigate the next week after his passing. We chatted and laughed about life and circumstances. I asked him, "Daddy, where would you like me to scatter your ashes?" and he answered, "Surprise me." He had a great sense of humor, lived large, generously, and with huge love for me and my siblings.

After the details were completed and he ate the last piece of chocolate fudge I brought him, he fell into unconsciousness. His last breath a day later was a giant inhale, just like his life.

My sister followed me around in a medicated haze for a couple of days while I sorted through the few bits of furniture, clothes, and personal items in his small single-wide mobile home.

Because he died with such short notice, plus it was Easter and the weather was so bad that weekend, no one but my sister and I were there for his funeral. We had a little deli sandwich picnic, huddled together in the freezing air, and scattered his ashes at his favorite fishing hole.

Despite the sense of urgency needed to get his affairs sorted out quickly, the sadness and general craziness and the short period of time I had left before having to head back to my home and work, I made time to meditate. Short, precious periods of time spent alone savoring the effect of this choice to look after myself.

I'd like to propose that often there are choices available to us in times of crisis or hardship that act as an opportunity to make coping more spiritually elegant. By elegant I mean that by making choices that are kinder to ourselves, we can create a softer 'landing.' A more elegant or refined 'landing' that helps us develop resilience and new habits. Our hearts can and will break, but not break into pieces.

I believe my softer landings have been supported by my lifelong willingness to seek solitude during times of stress. As a child, my solitude was a hiding place or a book.

I have had a bit of practice honing my coping skills. My parents began their divorce when my two siblings and I were toddlers. Growing up, this meant we spent our first decade of life separated from each other, shuffling back and forth between willing relatives, friends and acquaintances. I went to different schools mostly every year, in different locations depending on school-term living arrangements.

I recall often being a pawn in their angry game. Fueled by my father's alcoholism, there were unkind words and accusations from one about the other while being forced to take sides, cruel tricks designed to make the other look bad and suffer embarrassing public humiliation.

In retrospect, the most heart-rending was the emotional collateral damage to me and my siblings caused by my parents' desire to hurt each other.

I remember vividly the everyday smell of cigarettes and alcohol on my father's breath. It was normal for him to stop the car at the side of the road to vomit before stopping at a bar where I would wait in the car, wander around the parking lot or sit in the bar until he was replenished. I spent many hours as a young girl sitting quietly, drawing, reading or filling in coloring books while waiting in a back booth in bars that all looked and smelled the same. There were always kindly bartenders, bad neon lighting, sour, stuffy cigarette- and booze-soaked air, grubby floors, and jukebox music.

I developed a thick skin for inconvenient surprises and a relatively mature perspective for disappointments. I feel as if I was drawn naturally to actively create time to be alone after intense stress. This could be hiding away reading a book, taking a walk, sitting in a tree, laying hidden on my back in the tall grasses of a nearby field, sitting in a quiet corner of a random location. I trusted that being alone was safe, and where I could go to recharge my strength, and often, hope. I believe this early habit built a confidence for it that I brought into adult life.

Less than a year after my father died, my sister died of a drug overdose. I was called on the phone by a good friend of hers who explained that she had been discovered just a few moments earlier, dead in her bed. The police coroner had arrived and was arranging for her to be transferred to the morgue. I told her friend that I would be on the next flight I could get from London to her home in Hawaii.

My most immediate concern was that I had to break the news to my mother on the phone and do it before someone else did. I was standing alone on a bustling, noisy London street corner, inert with the gravity of the news.

I found a quiet, empty stairwell nearby and stepped inside to make my call. I will always be grateful for the strength, calm, and wisdom of my mother during that most difficult conversation. I can't even remember the words of the conversation, only how I felt afterwards. We knew that there was nothing we could do about what had already happened and we knew there was painful work to do in the following few days.

My mother and I decided that because of her failing health, I should travel alone to Hawaii to settle and organize my sister's affairs. My sister was a waitress at a local breakfast café and her chattels were modest and uncomplicated: an old car, some clothes, costume jewelry, and other small personal items. Her beloved cat would stay with her partner.

I arrived and drove straight to her house and was met by a houseful of some of her dear friends. People came and went from the house for hours, crying and laughing, telling stories, eating food and reminiscing. My sister's bedroom remained untouched for a couple of days except for her cat curling up for hours on her side of the bed where she died.

I got on with the now familiar and time-sensitive tasks and decisions associated with death. As her death was accidental and unexpected, I needed to unravel her every-day life and do what I could to close down any unfinished business. We celebrated her death in the Hawaiian way: gatherings, food, loving gestures and a beautiful Hawaiian burial at sea. There were four outriggers full of her friends wearing beautiful flower leis, and more people standing on the beach. Some of her ashes were scattered into the ocean along with petals and leis, singing and prayers. Because my mom couldn't travel and be there with us, I organized to capture the funeral ceremony live by cellphone. I held the phone wherever it needed to be, so she could hear every word and tribute.

The love and support shown to me by her friends, the caress of the breezes, the fragrance and splendor of Hawaii in March was like a soothing balm. I had a chance to examine and celebrate her life more meaningfully and compassionately through this experience.

The next day, I packed up her personal possessions in two large boxes and sent them by post to my mother's house. I put her few bits of costume jewelry in my purse.

When it was time to go, I carried the remainder of my sister's ashes back in a ceramic jar in my lap on the airplane to California for my mother and for an additional funeral service for friends and relatives on the mainland. I arranged for her memorial service to be in the same place we had held my father's. In that same favorite fishing hole, just a year earlier, was the last time I had seen my sister alive. The physical degradation of a young lifetime of hard drinking and drug use meant that every year she was still alive felt like we were given a secret gift. I remember toward the end of her life it took my breath away to look at how her body was changing. She struggled her whole life with drug and alcohol addiction, as did my father. I wish she would have hung around on this earth a while longer. She was forty-four, vibrant, creative, funny, and a true friend.

My mother had a disabling stroke the following year. She had suffered from depression after my brother's death and her health started to deteriorate even more after my sister died. She could no longer live alone, drive or do most of the little things we take for granted. Most important for her, the stroke meant the startling loss of her independence and privacy.

Another big challenge she faced was not having the finances to pay for the full-time care she now needed. I wanted to make an effort and see if I could help her stay at her home with the least amount of disruption. So, I often traveled back and forth from my home in London, staying for a week or two at a time. I shopped for her groceries online for delivery each week, hired (after she had fired) many housekeepers, gardeners, and people I selected to drive her to appointments, visiting nurses and physical therapists. I was getting exhausted and stressed managing it all from so far away and her situation wasn't improving. Something had to give.

After much research of the alternatives and a lot of soul searching, I decided I would have to more closely manage her care. There was no one else to do it and the finances weren't available for her to do it on her own.

It meant a huge leap of faith. I would have to re-imagine my international career and relationships, sell my home in London, buy a home in California, move her into my new house, and sell her home of forty-three years. It was hard for both my mom and me as we readjusted to living under the same roof. As people who have been through it know, taking care of an elder can be difficult, and a stroke can change your entire life in an instant.

Her health continued to get worse and she became more frustrated and despondent. I was torn between my love and loyalty for her and my desire for peace and harmony. She was often unhappy, complaining of boredom and disappointment. The effect of the stroke made her secretive and manipulative, with paranoid delusions.

She died after a short, painful, and unsuccessful treatment for leukemia. The experience of navigating a dying loved one through the US Healthcare system is something I don't wish on anyone. I am, however, grateful to have been able to look after her in my home until she died. Despite the stress and turmoil caused by taking on full time care of a parent with whom

I did not get along, I would still sign up for it again. Like most of us when we lose our mothers, we realize they are still here. In a sound, a mannerism, a gesture, a point of view. I am regularly gifted with coincidences that I am sure she is responsible for, whether it be found-money in the bottom of an empty purse or a profound insight or wisdom that keeps me safe or smart – just when I need it.

Earlier I referred to how I believe the way I have coped with crisis and hardship has been because I chose to trust myself in the face of it. This meant that I chose to step in and help and do my duty where I could, and then retreat to take care of myself. Retreat as an adult doesn't always mean disappearing – we can't always do that.

I began also to spread meditative moments – mindfulness - more broadly into daily life as I heard and read comments that resonated with me. "Breathe as if air was love itself," one teacher commented about the mind, body, breath connection. "If you are going to walk, walk; If you are going to eat, eat," said another about focus and intention. "The most precious gift we can give others is our presence," wrote the wonderful teacher, Thich Nhat Hanh. All inspirational words that link to everyday behavior.

Each death was an intense and unique experience for me, expected and unexpected at the same time. Each required that I wrestle unfamiliar physical and emotional responses and then make choices about how to proceed.

After some trial and error, meditation and mindfulness has proven to be the window I opened that has led me to the most personal benefit. Meditation is not always twenty minutes sitting down, it is a way of living. It is a simple awareness of breath, mindfully paying attention to my own responses and the world around me.

Meditation and mindfulness helps calm, support, and strengthen my resolve in times of crisis and chaos.

Meditation is a gentle discipline that still challenges me daily even after years of practice. The best way to describe what I do is to put it simply. I sit quietly for a time, focusing on my breath, with as much kindness and compassion for myself and others as I can muster. If I find myself distracted, I gently go back to my breath. Meditation over time has become a way of living. This has proven to be my well of resilience.

There are many ways to explore meditation and mindfulness and I needed to choose the path that is right for me. Step by step I figured it out. There is one constant: it doesn't happen until I actually do it! You must know that sitting still, quietly, breathing gently, without judgment or a goal can be very challenging, but every time I tried it, I began the process of strengthening the ease with which I managed the ups and downs of everyday life. As a result, I feel reduced stress and better responses to stressful situations, better health, better sleep, easier access to compassion for myself and others, objectivity and clarity.

Perhaps my childhood propensity for solitude has led me more naturally to my adult meditation and mindfulness practice. There is no doubt that this choice has supported my resilience. Resilience is ordinary, not extraordinary. It is not a trait that I particularly have, but a set of behaviors, thoughts and actions that have been awakened and developed in me. Step by step.

CHAPTER 9

COURAGE

Beverly McDonald

I am going to die. One sheep, two sheep, three sheep, four SHEEP! You're stupid for even trying this. You'll never sleep this way...

It's February and I haven't slept in six relentless nights. I feel lost, lost somewhere between life and death and I cannot reason with my mental roommate. All I can do is hide under my blankets with tears dripping down my tired and splotched red face and try, TRY to convince my roommate to give me rest.

My roommate isn't a new one. She has been there ever since I can remember being alive. My psyche has always been the bitter best friend I have never remembered inviting inside. She was the one that told me, "Oh, that's scary!!" and other times she reminded me of how utterly hopeless it was to even try new things. My psyche has always felt like much more than just my thinking mind: she appeared to have her own ideas, likes, dislikes, and opinions that I felt prisoner to, for if I didn't agree, I'd be punished with hateful self-talk or, sometimes, physical abuse.

I am on my death bed. This sleep will be my final flight into nothingness. My roommate demanded I listen as I laid in my bed shaking and convulsing uncontrollably. That was my cycle for six tumultuous nights.

On the seventh day, I couldn't take it anymore. I maniacally got dressed only to put on more clothes than I ever had in my entire life. As I made the elevator trip down fifteen floors to the freezing outside, I realized that my three layers were not enough and ran back in to grab a scarf for my face. One experience with a face full of frozen tears and icicle snot will teach you to cover your face. The temperature on my phone read 33 degrees Fahrenheit.

I rushed past busy Torontonians on their way to work and regular life to a wellness shop at Baldwin and Beverly. I felt lost. Overwhelmed. Confused. Sad. My mental roommate had been frantically reminding me of everything that's wrong with everything. *It's too cold here. What's that person looking at? Where is the damn trolley car?!* She decided right then and there that if we did not sleep that night, we were going to blow my brains out. I admit that this is confusing. It felt down-right crazy. Who am I taking orders from? Isn't it *me* just talking to *me* in there? We even went so far as to mentally arrange how I would find a gun and muster the courage. This fleeting thought was a solid plan in mere seconds. It felt like this disconnect of mind and *me* had finally come down to life or death.

When I arrived, the shop was closed, and I about dropped to my death bed - also known as the welcome mat. I collapsed into the doorframe and sobbed. I cried so hard that my stomach hurt. It was that deep guttural weeping that only your soul can muster. I felt broken.

A middle-aged woman about five feet tall and wearing barely a thermal rushed me inside. I thought I was dreaming when that being of seemingly clear white light had come around the back corner to the front door to let me in.

"Honey, are you ok?" She spoke softly and with a warm tone.

"I don't know. I don't know what's wrong with me. I haven't slept for six nights," I managed to squeak out between sobs.

With a look of compassion mixed with slight confusion, she said, "This must be your first Toronto winter, and it's a doozy. Here, honey, would you like some tea?"

"Oh, yes, my boyfriend and I moved here from California just a few months ago...I don't know what's wrong with me. The city feels so loud. I can't sleep. I'm so sad and I don't know why."

I had a boyfriend at the time. I didn't travel to Toronto alone. I met him when I was living and working as a tour guide in Amsterdam seven months earlier. He was on my tour and we instantly connected. I felt at the time that he was the reason I had traveled all the way to Europe, especially when I learned that he was from southern California, which is where I'm from originally. I had traveled my way through Europe searching for something and he felt like it. That's when I left Holland and jetted to his apartment in Los Angeles. His job would move the both of us to Toronto a few months later. When I packed up my two battered and well-traveled suitcases for the umpteenth time, my mental roommate came along.

The woman in the wellness shop looked at me again with tenderness, followed by the familiar look of sheer confusion as though I had three heads. I got this look a lot during my time in the northeast. Not many people move from California to Canada in the dead of winter on purpose.

She loaded me up with some herbal sprays and essential oils that were promised to calm me down and lull me to sleep. They were strong elixirs that went under my tongue: one spray in the morning and another right before bed. She also suggested I stop by the pharmacy next door and grab some vitamin D. I did and returned home exhausted and ready for a warm bath.

I did some research when I got home that day and realized that I was in a bad way physically. I was severely vitamin D deficient and it was actually driving me into psychosis. Growing up in a very sunny environment like California and then moving to the dead of winter where the sun is a ghost for months on end, I learned it was vital to take supplements for wellness. Now that I knew, I never missed a drop.

I cannot say that my mental roommate ever really stopped meddling in my life, though. Sure, she had dropped the incessant need to keep me awake at night and we didn't end up blowing my brains out like we had planned but the disconnect of mind and *me* only got worse. This disconnect grew to the point that I stopped being any type of social for fear of what I might *think* or say, and it started to physically disconnect me and make me feel outside of my body.

I started to notice that when people spoke to me, it felt like they were very far away from my physical body, even if they were right next to me. I tried to express my feelings to my boyfriend but even I admit that, at the time, I sounded pretty out there and crazy. Plus, he just wasn't experiencing the same things I was. He was going to work every day and interacting with people he knew in an office not too different from his office in Los Angeles. That was his normal. I had been an active, outdoorsy, avid hiker and biker that had never seen snow fall before and here I was in a frigid and damp city feeling like a fish out of water.

As the weeks went on, my disconnect got worse and worse. I felt so outside of my body, I couldn't function as a normal person and go to my reception job regularly. I was missing work far more than was appropriate and was met with only compassion and understanding by my bosses. It was a nice relief to be even slightly understood.

During my time at home, I started looking into podcasts for anxiety and googled things like 'I feel like I'm floating' which, of course, prompted a plethora of web md results that said I'm schizophrenic or worse. Then I found something about dissociative personality disorder and it caught my attention. That was it. That was how I felt. Disorders weren't new terminology for me: I had been diagnosed with panic and anxiety disorder when I was younger and occasionally still had episodes. When I saw that this disassociation was a coping mechanism for the panic and anxiety, I felt better. I finally had an answer that my mental roommate could understand.

I was still disassociating though. I still didn't feel like I could control the floating. The clinical answer did little more than give my mental roommate a bit more ammo to make me feel worthless. *Another thing wrong with you...great!*

I started picking up books, mostly from the Spadina Public Library or on google books. Any books, but primarily those with sequels so that I could stay in the story longer. I used to read a lot as a kid and always loved how the story drew me into another time and space. I also took up some grounding exercises (earthing and qi gong breathing) and found them to be very helpful but also difficult in my current state. I would have to perform my techniques many times throughout the day whereas reading allowed me to enter another world, to ground in that reality, instead of my own.

In the final two months of my life in Canada, I discovered The Four Agreements by Don Miguel Ruiz. This book changed my life. It felt like this book got to the core of me and made me question everything I thought I knew. What was odd was that I let it. The first agreement, *Be Impeccable with Your Word*, kick-started a mindfulness I could never give enough gratitude for. Being impeccable with my word to myself was the biggest game changer to date. I learned that I could ignore my mental roommate! I learned that she lies! The second agreement, *Take Nothing Personally*, freed up my nasty best friend even more! If she couldn't take every tiny thing personally, what was there for her to be upset about?! FREEDOM! The other two agreements and his following books iced the cake.

I let this book get inside me. I lived and breathed my new agreements and the world felt different. I was starting to see that other side of life, the one I had been reaching for since childhood, the side of life that isn't prisoner to an outdated belief system, the side that works with life instead of trying to control every piece of life that just isn't meant to be controlled!

I made a notebook with my new agreements and rid myself of old habits and ideas. I rewrote my belief system, so it looked and sounded the way I wanted it to be. I felt on top of the world! The problem was, I didn't feel I was *IN* the world. I was in a boring job, an unhappy relationship, a crazy climate (if it wasn't freezing, it was humid and miserable), and I was far away from my family. It was becoming harder and harder to continue existing in the same way I had been existing for many months. I felt myself changing and I wanted my partner to be on the ride, but he wasn't. He was on his own path of finding success in his career and that's what was important to him. Things were tense, and we just didn't seem to have much compassion left for one another. My time in Toronto felt over.

The opportunity to leave arrived the morning of October 24, 2015. I had an impulse to check my boyfriend's phone, which I can honestly say isn't something I've ever been into.

That evening I confronted him with my hands on my hips, tears in my eyes. "Who is she? And why are you messaging with her while you're working and ignoring me?"

"Why are you looking at my phone?" he said with a dismissive tone.

"Why am I here? Why did you bring me here? Just answer me this: do you want me to leave?" The tears were falling now.

After what felt like the longest pause ever, he said, "Yes."

That was it.

I left four days later.

That four days was amazing and terrifying all in one. The logistics to get myself, my stuff, and my cat home felt crushing. I had the time to say, hear, and think all that needed to be said, heard, and thought about. The relationship ended amicably. The work that I had been doing for myself wasn't integrated yet though. It's easy to *say* you're going to change your beliefs, ideas and tell your mental roommate to shut up but *doing* exactly that is tough! I had to be willing to look at myself honestly and not beat myself up along the path of change, which wasn't my strong point. I was talking to myself at an alarming rate and it felt like the conversations were getting even more two-sided. I had to constantly pull my attention back to the 'now' by doing my grounding exercises.

I left Toronto at 4 a.m. on a rainy and windy October 28th and never looked back. Leaving that life was strange. There I was, driving five thousand miles across the continent in a U-Haul with my cat and all my things. I was driving back to a house I hadn't lived in, and a family I hadn't seen, for four years. This was unmarked territory and my mental roommate was not letting me forget any part of my journey.

As I left Canada on the Rainbow Bridge which separates the two nations of Canada and the U.S., I felt…nothing. I still didn't have a lot of emotions. I was excited to get home but nervous as hell. Happy to be leaving Toronto, but terrified at what might be next. The first emotion I did experience was while standing in line to get my food at Arby's when I stopped on the second night in Lexington, Nebraska. I became overwhelmingly exhausted. It hit me like a freight train.

I settled back into my hotel room where I had gotten Belle (my cat) situated and I forced myself to eat as much as I could of my almost-cold roast beef sandwich and then I took a warm bath, as is my nightly ritual.

I felt restless, tired, uneasy, sad. What the hell had I just done?!

I missed the familiarity of my life in Toronto even if it was miserable.

I was returning to a family that didn't really know me anymore. What if this new belief system isn't strong enough to combat my old one? What if I had made a mistake?

I went to bed that night with almost zero success in falling asleep. I resigned myself to being awake and called my mom at about 3 a.m.

"Hi honey. Everything ok?" she said with a tired and frantic voice.

"No. What am I doing? What did I do? I have so far to go and I'm tired. I'm hurting. I can't do this." I started crying.

"Yes, you can. Do you want dad to fly out and drive with you?"

I heard this and something changed inside me.

"No, mom. I can do it. I have to do this. And I have to do it alone."

I did have to do this alone. I had done everything up to this point on my own and I couldn't stop now. I felt it: something was going to come of this solo trip and I had to get through it.

I knew that I'd be hitting another time zone that afternoon and if I started too early I would be exhausted around 2 p.m. and the hotel check-ins aren't until 3. I tried to force myself to sleep for as long as I could but my mental roommate wasn't having it. She forced me to get up and continue on my journey into Colorado. I once again felt the urge to 'do' something if this journey got any harder. This time, the mental plan was to drive my U-Haul off a cliff. It was clear my mind was still fragile.

Slowly, as I drove along Highway 70 into Colorado, my momentum came back as the sun came up. I was pretty much back to my normal self. Roommate meddling felt reduced to a minimum.

Driving into Denver, I hit a bit of rain but wasn't all that concerned about it. I wanted to go through the Rockies and had planned it so that I would, keeping in mind that it was late October and the weather would be a month or so away. Instead, the rain only got harder and the wind stronger. The snow caught me completely off-guard as I made my way up the grade into the mountains.

It was snowing, and REAL snow! I monitored my speed since I had never in my life driven in snow. We didn't have a car in Toronto; we relied on public transit or the occasional zip car. Towards the top of the mountain, there were cars pulled over, semis stuck, and it didn't look like conditions were getting any better. Reluctantly and possibly stupidly of me, I forged ahead. My choices as I saw them were either pull over, get covered in snow then be dug out later, or get through this as carefully as possible. I hunkered down and decided that I was getting us through this no matter what I had to do.

At the top of the mountain, traffic slowed to almost a stop. I applied very little pressure to my breaks. I immediately started to fishtail and slide sideways into the very small car in front of me that had nothing but a cliff to stop its (our) fall.

In that moment, I was overcome with sheer panic and clarifying calm. In that instant, my mind went quiet, my anxiety flew away, and my heart exploded into love.

My mental roommate was no longer with me. I instantly had the answers to everything. I started sobbing like a baby and quickly called my best friend, Mariela, who recorded our conversations and still has them which I am forever grateful for.

I then called my mom. Full of every emotion, I screamed into the phone, "Oh, my god! Oh, my god! Oh, my god! OH, MY, GOD, mom! Everything. Everything is beautiful, everything is potential! Jesus was a man! Just a man! Religion has it all wrong! Oh, my god! I

SEE…EVERYTHING!"

She was sobbing, "Oh honey, I want to hug you. I'm so happy for you. Now, you know who you are."

Hearing my mother's response should have been stranger to me but given that I was in infinity, it wasn't. It made perfect sense. Everything made perfect sense.

I was able to stop the car without incident and continue down the hill into Utah as planned. The girl who drove up that mountain was not the woman who drove down it. As quickly as the knowledge arrived, I did not lose this gift as I have heard others say might happen. I was wide awake. I got it. I got life. It made sense. I felt in my infinite space for hours, days afterwards and knew that I could call on the wisdom of this energy at any time.

I was changed at the core source level. I know that I was abruptly woken up at that time because I needed to be. I had been one of the walking dead, merely existing before this. I lived in fear of my mental roommate's wrath, my thoughts consumed with questions and fears like *Why are we here? What is the purpose? Holy shit, I'm gonna die.* I had threatened violence on myself on more than one occasion, and my higher self knew I would eventually take action if I didn't wake up. Even before my awakening, I knew I had lived many, many lives on this planet. I just felt it deep inside me and it has been confirmed by many mediums in my life. I feel now that this is my final life on this planet/in this dimension and it was vital that I wake up and not waste it. I realized I was misusing my gifts and was way off my path.

Having a quiet mind was a gift I never knew to ask for. I never knew that is was possible to live a life free of self-judgment, doubt, limiting beliefs and ideas. I thought I was supposed to do *this*, go to *that* college, buy *that* picket fence. I tried my hardest to 'fit in' and I never did. The effort resulted in me being miserable and almost wasting my life completely by taking it away. Following my heart and listening to my own inner wisdom has been what has allowed me to find this balance and happiness within myself.

CHAPTER 10

TRANSITIONS

J. Whitley

<u>Awakening</u>

It was not an epiphany but more akin to a slow undercurrent of self-hatred and pain that lasted for 28 years. My high tolerance for being in unhealthy environments trained me to stay versus recognizing I deserved better. The situation had to be so bad that I became hopeless and I knew that I could no longer exist in the status quo. I did not know how to make the fear and the sense of hopelessness abate. At that point, all I could do was let go and suddenly I awoke.

<u>Michigan</u>

I had lived in Western Michigan for two years at this point. It was very difficult to meet people when I first moved there at the age of twenty-four. Everyone I met was married with kids or on their way to a divorce. For two years, I joined sports leagues – soccer, softball, and volleyball – hoping to meet and develop a solid group of friends. After two years, I had not cracked the code.

On this occasion, my coed volleyball team decided to join a snow volleyball tournament which is essentially where you play six-on-six outside in snow. Yes, really. I was excited about the opportunity to travel and get to know this group of people. I had only played with the team a few months. We arrived on a Friday evening and checked in to our hotel and met up with some other teams at a social. It was about 9 p.m. and people began dispersing to rest up for tomorrow's games. A couple of people asked if I could drop them off at their hotel on the other side of the river just across the bridge.

After dropping them off, I realized that I had no idea how to get back across the bridge and to my hotel. In this pre-cell phone GPS environment in 1996, I was left to my memory and retraced my route. I was pretty tired after driving five hours to get here and I had no idea how to contact my other teammates. I drove around until I saw the bridge I had crossed.

Anxious to get home, I drove up towards the bridge. I was on a road that paralleled the bridge. What I thought, incorrectly, was that the road I was on would take me on to the bridge and back to my hotel. As I searched for the access point to the upper road, I did not pay attention too closely to my surroundings. It was dark due to poor street lighting and I could not see much ahead of me. The road was covered in snow. It was here that I saw before me a black abyss. I jammed on my breaks realizing that I was a hundred feet from the river.

My car slowly slid on the ice and into the river. I'm sure the slide was only a few seconds but it felt like minutes. I kept thinking that if I hit the brakes harder I would stop, but I did not. My car launched itself like a boat into the river and it floated with the current. As soon as my engine hit the water, it stalled. I could not open the doors or the windows. I was in disbelief and began to panic. It was minus-twenty degrees outside and I was trapped in my car sinking into the river.

As water filled up my car, I could feel the fight or flight take over my body. One thought came over and over in a mantra: *I will not die in Michigan. There is no fucking way I will die tonight.* I tried to kick out the front window, but it wouldn't give. I couldn't feel the coldness of the river. My adrenaline was at full force. I managed to stay calm and think. When the car was one-quarter filled with water, essentially to my seat level, I tried the door again and it opened as the depth of water equalized on either side of the car. The car immediately sank, ripping my jacket off.

I maintained focus and knew exactly what to do. I swam to the river bank where sheets of ice made it difficult to get out of the water. I used my wet hands to freeze onto the ice, so I could pull myself out of the water. I managed to get up to the road and with bleeding hands and wearing only a sweater and jeans. Ice began to form on my clothing and my face. There was very little traffic on a Friday night and the first few cars passed me by as if I was crazy. Finally, I was able to flag down a car. I began to hyperventilate as a driver pulled up. He thought I was trying to commit suicide and took me to the police station, where he worked as a psychologist.

At the station, I was wrapped in blankets trying to get warm, where I insisted I did not try to kill myself. I had just rescued myself out of a vehicle; I would not run into the middle of the road to try to get hit to kill myself. To keep me "safe," they threw me in isolation and didn't want to let me keep the blanket out of fear I would kill myself. I finally convinced one of them to give me a blanket as I could not stop shivering. Why they did not take me to the hospital is beyond me and still is to this day.

The police got hold of my team at the hotel and a few came to pick me up. Luckily, one was a nurse who heard what happened and immediately took my body temperature which was ninety-six degrees. Upon arrival at the hotel she blasted the heat in the room and wrapped me in blankets. My car was totaled but I was alive. I ended up having to pay for a dive team to remove my car from the river. I was so embarrassed, I did not play on the team again.

In the face of death, I evaluated my life in those few short seconds and it was clear that I was not where I wanted to be. I had really no social life despite my efforts. I didn't have that wingman to go out with to meet new people. I was the odd man out and it is always surprising to me how people do not reach out to newcomers when they are alone. The sense of isolation was overwhelming and I held on to work as a lifeline. On occasion, I would meet men and attempt to date them, but after three weeks with them I stopped because it didn't feel right. With no relationship and few friends, I was not happy but I'd become complacent with my situation. The job was great when I traveled but then I had to come home to Michigan.

LGBT What?

The hardest thing I've ever had to face is the fact that I am gay. The feelings I avoided were there since as long as I can remember. The first problem was not understanding that I could be attracted to the same sex and the second problem was in not accepting it. I knew that I would lose my family and the few friends I had because being gay was not right.

Growing up in a strict religious environment, thanks to my mom, I had a moral construct that ruled my conscious. Throughout my life, if my thoughts or actions veered from the accepted behavior, I believed that I would go to hell. My only reassurance was that if I conformed again and repented, then I would be saved. This caused me to avoid at all costs any feelings towards women. There were many sermons about not lying down with another man; the story of Sodom and Gomorrah was shared as an example of what would happen if such sins were committed.

I didn't know of anyone who was gay until I was 18 years old. His name was Jeffrey and he was ostracized on our campus. He was called "faggot" and physically knocked to the ground when he walked from his dorm to the school. His dorm room was damaged on a frequent basis. This seemed to fire him up as he took to roller skating topless with tight shorts around campus with Pride flags, which brought out the anti-gay sentiment even more. It was now clearly pervasive on campus and gay bashing became common and people were vocally more anti-gay publicly. Jeffrey was there for only one more semester.

In addition to attending a campus unwelcoming to gays, I joined a sorority where the Greek lifestyle in the 80's was even more straight-oriented and discriminatory. I did go out with several men but didn't partake in the hooking-up culture that was rampant on campus. It didn't occur to me until my sophomore year that women could be together. I had crushes on my friends and teachers, but I thought that meant I really liked them. I had none of these feelings towards men but thought I was a late bloomer.

My sophomore year of college, I was a resident assistant (RA) for over thirty students on the third floor of a ten-story building. I was really well liked by everyone in the building and I was sought out to assist more often than the other RAs. I was approachable and truly cared about the wellbeing of fellow students and they sensed that. One Sunday afternoon, a distraught girl showed up at my door. She was not on my floor but she said I was nice and heard good things about me. I knew her somewhat because she was going out all the time. So, I was a bit shocked when she said, "I'm gay," and began crying. My uninformed and naïve response was, "But you are always sleeping with men." I couldn't comprehend what she was saying. Her coming out to me filled me confused feelings and I felt uncomfortable. All the homophobic thoughts I was taught growing up came to mind while she was talking. I kept my thoughts to myself but realized that I really had issues with her lifestyle and was judging her.

Five years later in graduate school, I met Monica, a fellow grad student in my program. I had never hit it off with someone as quickly and soon Monica and I were inseparable. We even slept together most nights of the week. I felt so close to her and she to me. She would go out with guys on dates, on occasion have sex with them then come over and sleep with me. I didn't think anything about the closeness being abnormal. In fact, it felt normal. It was when she had to leave school due to personal reasons and went to Arizona that her loss was more devastating to me than it should have been. It was at this time I realized that I might be gay.

Because of my closeness to Monica, my fellow classmates started to ask if I was a lesbian. I said no and was mortified people thought I was. I began to date men or, worse, sleep with them to prove otherwise. I was miserable and confused. Shortly after I graduated I convinced myself I was just going through a phase.

Then the following year, I took a job in Western Michigan, a conservative town of forty thousand people. My coworkers were mostly from the area and regular church-goers. They would mock gay people and other ethnicities. Even though I lived in a larger city and also a college town there was no visible gay presence. At this point, I did not discuss my feelings but continued to develop attractions to women at work who were my friends. They openly discussed their disgust for gays and lesbians and they bragged about not knowing any. If I wanted friends, I needed to push myself further into the closet. I continued dating men, breaking up with them in three weeks, not able to find any connection with anyone.

I was depressed. The very thing I was taught to abhor, I now knew was me. I decided to go to a therapist and tried to work through my inability to accept I was gay. I was lonely and the few friends I had would reject me if I came out as gay. Every session began with me not able to express myself. My therapist seemed disinterested as our sessions were redundant. He prescribed me Elavil because I could not break the anxiety and fear. The drugs seemed to make me more depressed. After my car accident, I stopped therapy and Elavil because I was not making any progress. Truth be told, I don't believe my therapist could relate or had much experience with someone coming out. For two more years I struggled against the thoughts and, at age twenty-eight, I knew I could no longer go on with my life as it existed. I was hopeless. I contemplated suicide because I thought death would be better than the rejection I would endure from admitting I was gay. I cried with such a sadness. I grieved what I would never have: a husband, children, a "normal" life, my mom's acceptance, and the loss of friends. I thought about my brush with death a few years earlier and that I did not want to die in Michigan, but the person I was raised to be did die in Michigan. I knew that the only way I could live was to just give in and accept that I was gay.

Shortly thereafter, I had a work trip to Hawaii and I decided to go to a lesbian bar there. When the taxi driver dropped me off, he said, "Are you sure you want to be dropped off here?" as if I mistakenly picked this bar. I ignored him and got out of the cab and walked into the bar. There were mostly tourists there, about twenty people in total. I started talking to one woman from San Francisco and explained my situation about being closeted and inexperienced. She cautioned me that if I told people that it would be a turn-off as women like me mostly experiment then go back to men. Later that evening, there was a show of two women licking whip cream off each other. Not exactly a turn-on to me but interesting nonetheless. After the performance, my new friend called them over and she proceeded to put to tuck $45 worth of single bills into various areas of my clothing, so the two women would writhe over me performing a joint lap dance. This was the most self-conscious experience of my life. Mortification barely describes it. She laughed. Needless to say, as we left the bar, we made out and the bar patrons chanted our names. I knew at that moment, the first time I kissed a girl, what I had missed all my life. I never saw her again until twenty-three years later.

From that day forward, I was honest about who I was. I didn't exactly run around telling people but I did start to pursue relationships with women. I told some of my work friends. I was not allowed near their kids anymore and those friends eventually disappeared from my life. I came out to my mother much later and was in a serious relationship. She has not accepted me to this day.

The Job

Working at for the government in small town Michigan in the 1990's is a bit like going back to the 1950's. Think Peyton Place. All key leadership positions were held by white men over forty. I was frequently and openly propositioned by many of these high-ranking married men who promised me a promotion if I slept with them. I received sexist comments about my double "breasted" suits and one man would never look me in the eyes but always a few inches lower. I at first laughed this off because I'd never experienced such blatant objectification and it seemed surreal that this still existed. It felt harmless, yet belittling.

I remember the day I received a phone call from the Director of Operations at my work desk. It was after 5 p.m. and I was sitting at my office adjacent to the Front Office. Everyone was gone for the day. I picked up the phone and the Director said he was going to come upstairs and lick my ear in the most lascivious voice. It was the first time in my life I actually felt vulnerable and afraid. I grabbed my belongings and got out of there immediately.

Despite the male dominated culture, I was fortunate enough that my education and my work achievements enabled me to move in to a job that isolated me from the good old boy mentality. The job allowed me to travel two weeks out of the month to DC and around the world but I always came back to a place I didn't want to be.

I was complacent but not content. I felt trapped by debt from student loans and I did not know what I wanted to do, where to go, and had no confidence that anyone would hire me. Self-esteem and self-doubt kept me from asking for more.

Friends

In life, catalysts show up. I already had the near-death experience, the isolation due to no social circle, an unacceptable work environment, and I was an outcast from the community because I was gay. The more I refused to take action in my life, the worse things became. I was being given signs that I needed to leave but I ignored them and continued to tolerate unhappiness. Who would hire me? Where would I go?

The first catalyst in my awakening was my college friend from College. Lidija was living in New York City and once I told her I was gay, she said I needed to leave the lesbian wasteland and move. To show me what was out there, she asked me to come to New York for a long weekend and she would take me to the lesbian bars in the Meatpacking District. So, I flew out. She took me out to a bar notorious for celebrity sightings. It was called Clit Club. This was the first time I saw a lot of women pack a club. There were go-go dancers, DJ music, and your typical over-the-top New York scene, just for lesbians. Lidija's words were, "See what you are missing? Move the fuck out of Michigan."

Back at home, the second catalyst was when I met Gabrielle while playing soccer. She was comfortable with being gay, we were close in age, and she had a practicality and directness that was likable and undeniable. She was an affable Brazilian who believed there was goodness everywhere and if you looked for the bad you would always find it. She had found her way to Michigan as an exchange student and decided she would live in the US after graduating college. She always had a smile and a kind word for everyone. Gabrielle gave me the final kick that pushed me across the goal line in June of 2000.

I had turned thirty and spent six years at a place physically and emotionally unacceptable to me. I had just gotten back from New York. I had broken up with someone I was not attracted to but cheated on me. I find it strange that my self-esteem from the break-up could be impacted by someone I didn't want. Personally, I was upset by what happened and professionally, I had nowhere else to go. I'd reached the apex of my life in Michigan. As a result, I had decided to put in for jobs on the west coast, where I was originally from and understood the culture better. I fit in. I was called up for a phone interview for a job in Southern California. Gabrielle looked at me and said, "How badly do you want the job?" I said, "I really want to leave, and I feel like my life is wasting away here." She said, "Act like you want it and to buy a plane ticket and show up in person for the interview."

So, I did.

<u>Universe</u>

When you are on the right path, it's amazing how everything falls into place. What was a struggle every day in Michigan developed into everything aligning to pave my way to Southern California. June 2000 = miserable to August 2000 = new life.

My interview was scheduled and I bought an airline ticket, reserved a hotel, and rented a car. During my flight from Michigan, I was nervous but hopeful. I knew no matter what happened, I could not be here anymore. When I landed in my new home, having done so once before, I experienced the exhilaration and excitement of seeing the amazing skyline, the bay, the sail boats and then the experience of almost grazing the tops of buildings as the plane gently set itself down on the tarmac. As the plane taxied to the gate, I felt like I had something to look forward to for the first time in a long time.

I drove to the hotel and checked in. I was too nervous to sit by myself in the room, so I went downstairs for the hotel's happy hour. I started talking to a woman at the hotel who was moving here. She was house hunting and gave me her number. She said let her know how things go and she could help me find a place.

The next morning, I showed up ten minutes early for the interview. I sat in the lobby in the small office of five people who scoped me out from their offices. I was led down the hallway to meet my interviewer who gave me no positive vibes. My interview was only thirty minutes and there were very few questions. I didn't know how it went. On the way back to the airport, I had enough time to drive around before I flew back to Michigan. I felt that I had taken the first step of moving forward with my life no matter what happened. In Southern California, I felt none of the oppression or stagnancy that enveloped my life in Michigan.

Two days later, I was offered the job. The interviewer later said that me flying out for an interview was what got me the job. I contacted the woman I had met at the hotel, who happened to find an apartment and there was vacancy coming up in the building. She convinced the landlord to rent me the property without meeting me. My Dad, who hadn't visited me in six years, offered to fly out, help me pack up my belongings and drive me to Southern California. Everything fell in line.

The Trick is to Keep Breathing

In retrospect, I let things get so bad and was miserable for so long that I wonder why I could not take action. Why had I tolerated so much and could not find a way out of it? Unfortunately, I've repeated the same behavior in another job, another relationship, and in living situations but each awakening process is quicker. A part of the process is in recognizing that if something doesn't feel right then it's not right.

Moving to California felt right. I arrived the weekend after Pride. The flags were still up in the gay neighborhood. I felt for the first time that I did not have to be closeted and I had a chance to live the life I wanted to live. I knew no one but I made it a point to go out and meet people, join a soccer league, join a pool league, pretty much anything. Within months I had several friends and started a new life that was significantly happier than the life I had in Michigan. Within a year I had a girlfriend and a stable personal life. All because I had the courage to leave my miserable life behind and ask for more.

All was not perfect. The job I took to move to was a nightmare and three years later, I had to take a pay cut to get away from it. That decision resulted in me being far more successful in the long run. This again validated that awakening is an everyday process and we need to check in with ourselves when things don't feel right.

Finding the ability to leave bad relationships gave me another opportunity to practice awakening. I stayed five years too long because I did not want to hurt her feelings. Another, I stayed with despite being cheated on three times. I'm far from a perfect model of practicing awakening. It's a challenge to fight for my happiness as I am afraid that things will get worse despite a lifetime of proof of the opposite. Every time I become awake and do something for myself, my life gets better.

For me, my awakening will be with me my entire life. I still struggle with moving forward when I'm not in the right place. At times, I go to great lengths to stay in that struggle, either ignoring it, rationalizing that I'm fine, or watching Netflix. But deep down I can't avoid the awakening. It's a part of me and if I pay attention it will constantly move me forward to a better place. "The trick is to keep breathing," to quote my favorite Garbage song.

CHAPTER 11

FORGIVENESS

JR MacGregor

Every single thing I did growing up was so that someone would love me or pay attention to me.

I grew up in a middle-class home, a happy and creative child. It wasn't until I was about seven or eight that I realized that something was different about my family, that I learned what an alcoholic was. To a young girl, my dad was a bright light, filled with kindness and so much fun to be around. He was also a compulsive gambler and an alcoholic. In my younger years when my dad would disappear, my mom would say that he was away working. As I got older, I realized that "work" really meant a binge and that we had no idea when he would return. Sometimes, he would be gone for weeks at a time and we wouldn't know if he was dead or alive.

His disappearances would usually end the same way. I would be woken up by him crying at my bedside saying that he was home and was so, so sorry. He promised that he would never leave or drink again. I would always forgive him, not because I did or even had the capacity to do so at such a young age, but because I was so afraid that if I didn't, he would be upset again and leave, and it would be my fault. I was desperate for him to stay.

But he always left again. Sometimes it was weeks, sometimes a year. It was eerie how often I would think, "He is really better this time," and he would leave the next day. I started to wonder if it was somehow my fault and that I was causing it by my thoughts alone, like I had that control over him.

I became the peacemaker within my family trying to keep my brother's and mother's spirits high and to keep my dad happy so that he wouldn't leave again. This kind of people-pleasing attitude went full blown when I became a teenager. It was not a good combination with boys.

My identity was defined by whichever boy I was "in love" with at the time. If he was interested in a certain band, I would run out and buy every one of their CDs. If he dressed a certain way, so did I. I would obsess about ways I could run into him, even skipping school and wandering around places he would hang out. My sole focus would be about making these boys like me and I was desperate for their love and attention.

Plus, I lied. Now this wasn't exclusive to the boys I was in love with, it was also to my family, friends. I don't remember when I started to lie but it was definitely second nature to me by my late teens. I never lied because I wanted to hurt anyone. In contrast, I usually lied because I wanted other people to feel good or not worry about me. I can remember telling my mom stories about the high school quarterback flirting with me my first week of high school when I was really eating lunch in the bathroom on my own. She had enough to worry about with my dad and I didn't want her to have to worry about me, too.

It was also a way to control and manipulate a situation to get what I wanted, and what I wanted more than anything was to be loved. I would embellish stories to make people laugh or invent situations that I felt made me look 'better" than I actually was. In high school, I would make up boyfriends who, of course, lived out of town because my friends were all dating. I didn't want to be looked at as weird or unlovable because I wasn't dating. I would daydream and imagine a funny scenario that "could have" happened on the bus and tell it like it was fact to make my friends laugh. I never felt good enough on my own and I felt that these lies made me a more interesting person and more worthy of love.

I dated a little bit in my late teens but never really fell hard for someone until I was twenty and I met Ben.

I think I might have audibly gasped the first time I met him. I had moved away but was back in town for a wedding and he was one of the musicians. He was so charismatic, charming, confident, and handsome and we instantly became friends. He was interested in another mutual acquaintance at the time, but that didn't stop me from obsessing about him from afar. When the opportunity came for me to move back to my hometown, and where he was from, I took it instantly.

Within a few months we started dating and I was head over heels in what I thought was love. He was such a bright light and made me feel beautiful, capable, and loved. Early on, he started surprising me with flowers, presents, and letters professing his love. I couldn't believe that somebody THIS great could feel that way about me. Then his dark side came out.

After our first month, he started to become obsessive of where I was and what I was doing. I would get angry calls if I wasn't home by the time I said I would be. He would show up at my house to make sure I was home when I said that I was. He constantly drilled me on the people I would go out with and made me feel guilty for having male friends. It was subtle at first and easily mistaken for passion. I convinced myself that he wanted to know where I was all the time because he cared so much about me. He wanted to be with me all the time because we were so in love.

What I thought was passion clearly was obsession. He was constantly checking up on me, accusing me of everything from cheating on him to being on drugs. He would read my diary, listen in on my phone calls and even went through my garbage. Sometimes the interrogations would go all night with him screaming at me, insulting me, grabbing me and shaking me. A few times I even admitted to things I didn't do just for some peace, just so it would stop.

I knew pretty quickly that this wasn't what a healthy relationship looked like. My gut was screaming to get out as soon as possible, but, instead, I thought that in time he would grow to trust me, and his insecurities would go away. More than anything I wanted to be loved.

During our whole relationship, I felt like I was watching myself in a movie. Who was this girl? Why was she putting up with this? I felt so much shame at what I was becoming, and what and who I was giving up in this process. I never thought I would get into a relationship like this. I thought I was a strong woman. But here I was, like a cliché, thinking I could change him, that I could love him enough to heal the hurt from his past that made him this way. Because there was so much potential: Oh, what he COULD be, what WE could be.

While much of our time was dark, of course there was also light, and when he was happy it felt like the sun. Looking back on it, it is incredible that one person could make you feel so good and loved one minute and like a piece of trash the next. It was easy to get addicted to the drama and the passion but what I thought was passionate love was actually abuse.

Then one day, he decided to go back to school and moved away. Within a few weeks he was gone and I was heartbroken. For weeks all I did when I came home from work was cry and yet my soul felt relieved that I didn't have to be on egg shells anymore. I felt like I could take a full breath without being questioned about needing air in the first place. Since he had been by my side every day for over a year and I had given up most of my friends, I also felt incredibly alone.

Every month or so, he would drive twelve hours to come and visit or I would fly to him and we would spend a few days together. I think they were the closest thing to a "normal" relationship that we ever had. I thought that maybe after he graduated, I would move to the coast and we could have our happily ever after. No more controlling, no more interrogations, just all the shiny good parts of him.

Then I got pregnant.

I took the test, alone in my tiny apartment after my period was a few weeks late. We had had a couple of scares before and I just assumed that this would be another one. I peed on the stick, fully expecting to come back in three minutes and have it be negative. It wasn't. My stomach sunk. I sat down and started hyperventilating. How could this have happened? We were careful, weren't we? My mind began to race. On one hand, I was way too young for this. I had a bachelor apartment, no education, a minimum wage job. I had just finished upgrading and was getting ready to go to college.

A small bit of me thought maybe we could make it work. Our families would help and would love this baby. It would be challenging but people had done it before, why couldn't we? My heart was trying to fool my soul. I knew that having this baby could mean I would remain in a toxic relationship for the rest of my life. I would never be free from him.

This was a first pregnancy for me, but not for him. One of his previous girlfriends also got pregnant and had had an abortion. He told me that she had done it without his consent, how "against" it he was, and how much it hurt him. I didn't expect him to be happy when I called, but I didn't expect the response I got.

"Hey! How are you doing?" he answered cheerfully.

"Not so good," I managed to choke out. "I just took a pregnancy test and I'm, I'm pregnant."

"What? Are you sure?" He answered, sounding in shock. "Have you been to the doctor yet?"

"No, not yet," I replied.

"Well you need to go to the doctor right now. I think there is a pill that you can take, like an abortion pill. You've got to get to the doctor right now, I am not messing around," he threatened. "Are you sure it is mine?"

My response was a mixture of laughter and pure anger. I had never been unfaithful to him, even when he first moved and had cheated on me. "Of course, I am," I managed to spit out. "And those kinds of pills have to be taken within the first day or two."

"No, there is something, I am sure of it. Go to the doctor right now and then call me back," he demanded.

I went to a nearby walk-in clinic. Right where you check in there was a big sign saying that for ethical reasons Dr. So-and-So wouldn't prescribe the morning after pill. Right away, I felt shame and judgement and the beginning of other people having a say in my body and future. Thankfully, that was not the doctor on duty but the one who was confirmed what I already knew: that it was too late for any kind of pills. He coldly gave me the number for pregnancy counselling and an abortion clinic and left the room. When I told Ben what the doctor said, he was very upset.

"I am not ready to be a father. I just started school and my whole future is ahead of me," he said quietly.

Our conversation quickly turned into all the reasons why he wasn't ready to be a dad, how it would get in the way of his future, how we couldn't offer a child any kind of life.

"I think you should have an abortion," he said quietly.

I was shocked. Having an abortion was not even on my radar. I had actually privately judged friends for doing so, so how could I possibly even consider it? I told him I needed some time to think things through.

I ended up going to pregnancy counselling. They went through all the different options with me and were non-judgmental and kind. I left still feeling unsure but was thankful to have had someone to talk to who wasn't involved. I told a couple of co-workers whose reactions ranged from verbal support to bringing in prenatal vitamins. I desperately wanted to talk to my family about it, but I didn't want them to be disappointed in me.

I finally made the decision to have an abortion. I booked an appointment for a few days later and Ben flew down to be with me. The night before my appointment, I tried desperately to get "permission" to get out of it. I cried, and pleaded, and explained how it was against what I believed was right. There was such certainty from Ben that this was the only option and he became exasperated by my change of heart. We stayed up all night debating it, but I couldn't do it. I missed the appointment. He was terrified. He flew back the next day pleading with me to change my mind, reminding me of all we would lose and how he wouldn't be able to come back again.

I called my Mom and told her. I had wanted to keep this from her so she wouldn't be disappointed or think less of me. But I needed my mom. She knew in my voice that something was wrong right away.

"What is wrong, love?" she asked with a concerned tone. I burst out crying and wasn't able to speak. After a minute of her assuring me that everything was ok, she guessed it.

"Are you pregnant?"

"Yes," I sobbed. "I am so sorry."

"Oh honey, it's ok. Is it Ben's?" she asked. I squeaked out a yes and all she said was, "I didn't think he had it in him," trying to lighten my mood. I burst out laughing for the first time in ages and took a deep breath of relief. It was out. She still loved me. I wasn't on my own anymore. I told her about everything that had transpired over the last couple of weeks. Once I was finished, her advice shocked me

"I think you were right and should have the abortion," she said gently.

My first instinct was sadness. No, not her, too! I also knew she would only be thinking about me in this situation and I heard her out. She knew Ben. She had witnessed how I had changed since he came into my life and although I hadn't told her what he had done, she knew what a future with him would look like. She offered to fly to town and come with me so I wouldn't be alone. I re-booked my appointment and Mom booked her flight.

I drew strength from having my Mom there. Although I felt very sad, I didn't have the same doubts the night before like I had last time. The morning of my abortion, she gave me a necklace to wear that had a rune on it that stood for strength. We took a cab to hospital not knowing what to expect. I was afraid there would be people picketing or calling me a baby murderer as I walked in. In reality, it was just a wing in the hospital under a different name and no one was around. For security reasons you had to be buzzed in, but once in, it looked like another section of the hospital.

I was given a hospital gown, fit with an IV and Mom and I were brought to a cubicle area to wait. It had sheets on either side, makeshift dividers. There were women on either side and one of them was crying and scared.

The other had her own kids with her and was in "mom mode" trying to keep her kids behaved and oblivious to what was really going on.

A nurse came over and called my name and I stood up. My mom gave me a hug and offered again to come in. Part of me wanted to take her up on it. I was scared and didn't want to be alone, but I didn't know what to expect from the procedure itself and didn't want her to have that memory.

I sat in a room by myself with two nurses. One started to make some small talk with me which felt strange but also distracting and comforting. We talked about the weather and how it seemed busy in the clinic. She smiled and said they were usually busy there. She went on to explain that one in three women would have an abortion in her lifetime, which shocked me. The knowledge that so many women had gone through this before me both saddened and comforted me.

The other nurse gave me some medicine through my IV that she explained would make me a little woozy but would help ease any pain and make me not remember it as much. I didn't question it. The doctor came into the room and started to talk to the two nurses. He said a quick hello and explained briefly what would happen during the procedure.

"Let's get started, then," he said matter-of-factly. He sat at the end of my bed, my feet in stirrups, and one nurse joined him. The other nurse held my hand and I held onto hers for dear life as the procedure began. I shook with fear.

It was more painful than I expected. During an abortion, you have contractions like you do in labour. The pain gave me something to focus on rather than on my fear. The experience was surreal. I felt like I was watching it as a movie, that it was not actually happening to me. I kept my eyes on my own hand clenching the nurse's. She whispered encouragement and comfort to me, even stroking my hair and forehead when I had some complications and more doctors were called in.

All of a sudden, there was a team of people around me during the worst moment of my life. They ignored me and talked amongst themselves using medical jargon that I am still not familiar with. I looked at the nurse holding onto my hand and she reassured me that everything was going to be ok. Inside, I was panicking: *Is something serious happening? Am I dying? Maybe I deserve this for going through with the abortion.* While my mind wandered to terrible places, the doctors were able to get the procedure done. I had no idea how long I was in there; it seemed like it was just minutes and hours at the same time. The nurse walked me back to the waiting area where my Mom was waiting anxiously and said, "She did a great job." That felt so strange: it's the kind of thing the dentist would say to a parent. I got dressed quietly and we left.

We couldn't get a cab so we ended up taking the bus home. I looked around at all the strangers feeling like they could see through me and knew what I had just done. Mom and I sat in silence most of the way while I tried to sort out the feelings inside. I expected to feel sadness. I expected to feel guilt. I was surprised that what I felt that first day was a sense of relief. Relief that it was over and more than anything, relief that I didn't have to have Ben in my life forever. I wasn't going to be bound to him through a child. I had an out.

We got back to my apartment and I crawled into bed and Mom and I just had a quiet day. She called my boss to say I was ill and would be away for a few days. She made me soup and we ordered take out. It was as if I was home sick from school instead of just having gone through an abortion.

I called Ben to tell him about how it went. He knew Mom was coming down and I assumed that he would be waiting by the phone to ensure I had gone through with it this time. I imagined how he would comfort me and we would cry together. There was no answer. That evening was much of the same. Mom and I talked and watched some TV. I would call him and there would be no answer. I went to sleep worried that something was wrong with him, that the grief was too much for him and he was dealing with it in solitude. I woke up the next morning to his call. He sounded cheerful and nonchalantly said, "Hey, how are you? I see you tried to call yesterday, what's up?"

"What's up?!" I managed to get out behind gritted teeth. I was crying now and choked up. "Where were you yesterday?"

He got defensive right away. This wasn't how our relationship worked. He was the controller. He could demand things of me but not vice versa.

"Out," was all he cruelly replied. "What's the problem?"

I honestly don't remember what I said next or the words I used to remind him that I had had an abortion yesterday.

"Ohhh, I forgot that was yesterday. I went out last night with some friends," was his reply.

He "forgot." You forget items on your grocery list. You forget to grab your keys when you are heading out the door. You forget phone numbers and postal codes. You don't forget someone you love going through the hardest thing they have ever gone through and the termination of a pregnancy that you co-created.

Those words changed my life forever. They were the beginning of my awakening. I was used to him being cruel, lying, manipulating, so it certainly wasn't the worst thing he had said to me. I knew in that instant what I meant to him. I finally knew I was never going to be able to change him and that I deserved so much more.

I also knew that I needed to stop lying – to other people and to myself. That if a particular situation or scenario wasn't shiny, perfect, and fun then it wasn't my responsibility to make it that way. I also worked through a process of recognizing that I only wanted people in my life who would love me through the dark stuff, too, and if my life was crappy and boring they would love that, too.

Ben and I only talked on the phone a handful of times after the abortion. I saw him one more time after I was finished school and dating someone else. He was filled with smiles and tried to kiss me, telling me how much he missed me. I stopped him and told him he should leave. And he did. That moment solidified a feeling of being on the other side of my awakening – a feeling that I had closed that chapter and could say "no" to behaviors and people that didn't support me in loving, kind, and healthy ways.

On the outside, life went back to normal, albeit a new sort of normal. I slowly made new friends and learned to really value and cherish those relationships. I started mending the relationships that I could and working on myself and really trying to find out who I am and what I like. So many years of mirroring other people (especially the men I was interested in) left me really unsure of who I was. I worked hard at finding my voice again and then becoming unafraid of using it after being silent for so long. I fought the urge to lie and be more "interesting" and concentrated on being truthful.

The emotional healing of the abortion took much, much longer. I think the misconception is that people who have abortions are irresponsible and uncaring, that they have an abortion and go back to their former lives, never thinking of their unborn child. I can tell you, even after almost fifteen years, I still think about it often especially around the anniversary of the abortion itself. You feel filled with guilt when your friends have trouble conceiving on their own. You feel filled with shame when your friends who have been adopted are "so thankful that at least their parents didn't have abortions." You feel ashamed when members of your family support anti-abortion, having no idea that someone they love went through one. It is this massive, impactful event in your life that you just can't talk about without judgement.

It took almost ten years before I really forgave myself and, in a full-circle moment, it came from a lesson from my father. He never was able to give up drinking and passed away quite young. A year after he died, I learned about a mistake that he had made when he was young that led to his own journey of guilt, shame, and abuse. He was never able to forgive himself and created this cycle of self-punishment that impacted everyone around him. It brought such clarity to me and a level of understanding and kinship to him that I didn't have when he was alive. In forgiving him and seeing his humanity, I saw my own and forgave myself.

Fifteen years after my abortion, I ended up pregnant again. This time in a healthy marriage of almost ten years with a man who respects and really loves me, a man who knows all the dark parts of my past and loves me anyway, as I do him.

Our pregnancy was a surprise. Even though I had forgiven myself, I had this underlying feeling that I wasn't meant to be a mother. I felt that I had given up my chance as a mother when I had my abortion. With all the women struggling to get pregnant, I felt I didn't deserve another chance. Thankfully, God/the universe knew better.

A friend of mine who had had an abortion and had a child years later said to me, "You never really deal with the guilt of your abortion until you have a child and look in his or her eyes. Then you realize exactly what you gave up." That never left me and terrified me during my pregnancy.

When my son was born, I didn't feel that at all. Instead of sadness and guilt, I felt an overwhelming amount of gratitude and love to both my unborn baby and Ben for the tough roles they had to play in my life to get me to this moment, to help me become the woman and mother I was meant to be. Being the best version of myself and serving my family and friends with love is the greatest way that I can honor my mistakes and the life of my unborn child.

I have been asked if I regret getting the abortion. The answer is no. Only someone who has gone through it can understand that it was both the worst and best decision I have ever made. I regret getting pregnant in the first place and should have taken extra precautions, but I don't regret my decision, as hard as it was. I do wonder what kind of woman I would have become if I hadn't had it. Would I have ever stopped lying? Would I have stayed with Ben and put up with an abusive relationship all these years? Would that abuse have passed on to our child? Would I have had the courage to leave? Would I even still be alive? In this way, this crisis moment really was exactly what I needed to propel me forward into an awakening, and into so much personal growth. It has brought me to the place I am today.

All I really know is that if a single thing had gone differently, my son wouldn't be here. He is full of light, joy, kindness, and goodness and is the greatest love and blessing of my life. Because of my awakening, he will be raised in a house with unconditional love, honesty, compassion, and forgiveness.

CHAPTER 12

FAITH

Lynn Kay

Taking the First Step

The skies were a magnificent crystal-clear blue, the sun was shining bright as it usually does in San Diego, California, and my heart was beating a hundred miles an hour. I had signed up for this. I was able to raise the money (as they said I would), and other people raved about the experience, so why was I so hesitant? Was it because my self-confidence was so low it was buried six feet underground? Maybe it was because I didn't think I was worthy of living. Or was it something else? Although I knew I wanted to get back to the positive, happy, light-hearted person I knew I was, maybe it was the fear of the unknown, of wanting my life to change and yet being afraid of what that may mean. I desperately wanted to regain my sense of self-worth and be happy again, not only for me but for my five-year-old son, too.

As I sat in my car praying I would find the answers to those questions, I started preparing myself to make my way through the crowd and into the auditorium. There were hundreds of people milling around, so I did my old self-talk thing. I knew it well, for throughout my entire life (about 80 percent of it), I've always had to do almost everything alone and attending this event was no different. I took a deep breath, plastered on the Everything's Great smile, exited the car, and graciously nodded, smiled, or said, "Hi," as I made my way through clusters of people and into the building.

I found a seat, midsection, center, so as to not draw attention to myself. Yet, on some level, being there felt a little familiar. It wasn't a strong awareness or a déjà vu kind of feeling. It was more like I could sense the energy in the room, and it was mostly positive. I laugh now as I realize we probably all had our Everything's Great faces on.

As I sat there waiting for the event to begin, I couldn't help but wonder, *What had happened to that positive, strong, spiritual, fun-loving, happy-go-lucky woman I used to be – where the hell was she?* Why had I chosen to hide her? Why did I allow the men's words and actions of my past relationships to demean and belittle me to the point of thinking that I wasn't worthy of living?

Thus began the magical three-day weekend that was about to propel me back, and awaken a deeper sense of knowing within me. I like to call it Reclaiming the Power Within Me.

> ### *"When nothing is sure, everything is possible."*
> #### ~ **Margaret Drabble**

Before I get too far ahead of myself, let me give you a little background into how I ended up at this three-day event.

My life seemed to be wonderful: I had a beautiful son who I had wished for my entire life, and a good job, yet I found myself in the aftermath of yet another disabling and enabling relationship. I was unprepared, devastated beyond words, and questioned whether I should throw myself off my second-storey balcony, all while wondering if it would make any difference.

Over the next few difficult months, I regularly talked to my sisters and two of my nieces. Thank goodness, I have a great family support system! My niece, Karen, had recently completed this life changing three-day course. She was encouraging me to do it too, telling me how magnificent it was and how it would change my life, too.

Karen described the event as a powerful way of letting go, of seeing a new way of looking at things, and of having an experience like no other she had ever had. "That's all great," I asserted yet I was still skeptical and wondering what exactly goes on at this three-day event. Karen told me that the three days were not easy. In fact, she affirmed, "You will cry, you will be challenged, and it will definitely push you to step up and speak out in your life." Although I was hesitant, I told her I would do it and called the coordinator as soon as we hung up.

Thoughts rushed through my head: *Did I really want my entire life to change?* I don't know about you, but when someone tells me, 'This will change your life,' I start thinking, *Wait, is my life really that bad? Do I really want everything to change? What does that mean?!* As I contemplated whether or not I was really ready and, more than that, willing to change my life, I knew I had to do something or my life was not going to get any better.

Courage: Feeling the Fear and Doing It Anyway

As the nervous tension rumbled through my body and sweat dripped from my face, I swallowed hard, dialed the event's registration number, and tried to breathe as it rang through. An extremely nice person answered the phone and, as my quiet voice cracked, I inquired about the three-day program. The woman on the other end seemed so happy to help me. Her energy was vibrant, and I nearly sensed a ray of joy in my own energy as I spoke to her. Just talking to her, I started feeling better. I was ready to commit, and I exclaimed, "I'm doing the program." She then proceeded to tell me the cost. My heart sank. My thoughts started racing. I told myself that this wasn't for me, that I'd never be able to afford it. Then quickly something inside me said, *Lynn, you're going through another bad break-up. Is this the life you really want? Do you really want to feel this way for the rest of your life?*

Then something fascinating happened. The woman on the phone started telling me that as part of the program, the call we were on was actually the beginning, the first step in the three-day program. She strongly encouraged me to fully commit to the program and to myself, and to take a stand, knowing the money would be there. I sheepishly agreed and as I hung up the phone, a rush of despair came over me. I heard myself say, "This is impossible!" Prior to these relationships, and throughout most of my life, I had always had pride in myself on having unwavering faith. At this moment, however, I just felt helpless. As I placed the phone on the receiver, with tears in my eyes, I cried out, "Oh, no! What I have I just gotten myself into?"

I only had a few days to pay the balance for the event and honestly, to this day, I do not recall exactly how the money came to me. What I do know is that something that woman said triggered a spark of magic in me and I was able to make the payment – in full! I had done it and I was on my way to attending this magical three-day event that would ultimately change my life.

First Comes Love and Ignoring Myself

On the first day of the event, the group spent some time getting to know each other and we had the opportunity to tell each other why we were there and what we wanted to take away from this program. As I sat there listening to others talk, my mind wandered, and I started to think about why I was there and what I expected. My thoughts took me right back to all my past romantic relationships. Maybe I kept choosing to be with addictive-type personalities because of my father, who drank. My father was not a drunk, in my eyes. In fact, he was a quiet, loving, gentle soul who had had a terrible childhood. He quit school at a young age, lied about being 18 when he joined the military, then started drinking to forget. Maybe there was something to that: it felt like the men in my past relationships did love me, and they weren't physically abusive. They all, however, had a 'quiet' addiction or a controlling type of personality. In many of my relationships I felt criticized and demeaned, was lied to and cheated on. Was it really about them, or me? Why was I so blind to not see that I was the one who had allowed myself to be treated unfairly, cheated on, lied to, and painfully criticized? I remembered that there were moments in all these relationships, when that still, small, gentle voice inside me wondered why I had chosen these men. A feeling of intense truth overwhelmed me, and I had to wonder: why did I continue to ignore that voice?

I remember being extremely happy before each intimate relationship and so this one was no different. I was enjoying my new home in California, loving my life, dancing, being at the beach, soaking in the sun, and having a whole new life adventure! That's when it happened. One lovely hot starry summer night, I was out with friends and there he was.

This new guy was handsome, smart, and his smile was magnetic. I did my best to hold back and yet a part of me jumped all in, feet first! I'm not certain that we ever really dated, we pretty much just hung out, and then I started spending time at his place. I was over the moon when he told me he loved me first and felt somewhat surprised that a mature, attractive man with a good paying job told me he loved me! Things moved quickly and within six months, we had our own apartment and were living together.

Within the first few months of this relationship, that still, quiet voice in my gut was whispering, *You know he's not right for you. Do you call going through a drive-through for fast food a date? Why are you staying in this relationship?* "He said he loves me," I kept telling myself. And yet I wanted to know why I wasn't listening to my gut feelings, to that quiet small voice whispering within.

As I pondered that thought, my attention was quickly jerked back to reality and the sound of the monitor calling my name. My heart raced, my palms were clammy, and by body wanted to slink down under the seat in front of me. While I had been listening to everyone else share, and was remembering my own story, I realized that I had made a choice. I was the one who chose to ignore my feelings. I was the one who decided to stay in this relationship and all those similar past relationships. It was now my turn to explain why I was at this event. My knees buckled under me as I stood up and began to tell the room my heart-wrenching story. Many people identified with me; they truly understood and sympathized with my situation. Although it was nice to be heard and recognized, all I really wanted was the feeling of dread inside me to go away. I wanted to learn to listen to and trust myself, to regain my power, and most of all to feel joy and be happy again.

Eyes Wide Open: Holy Moly, What Just Happened?

When we were all done sharing, the speaker said, "Those were all nice stories. Now are you ready to tell yourself a different one?" He went on to say that we tell ourselves things all the time, every day, and we choose to have the stories hurt us, matter to us, and make us feel a certain way, even if we are not consciously aware of it. We tend to have strong opinions about what happened, become immersed in it, and deeply attach ourselves to our stories. We all realized that stories can be small or big, simple or elaborate, filled with joy, laughter, and love, or full of drama, grief, hatred, despair, and anger. I had to admit that this concept of stories was starting to make sense to me.

With this new-found information, I went home that night and thought about *my* story, all my past relationships, and what really had happened. Did I ever really love all those men? I knew I loved being in a relationship, having someone love me and provide companionship in my life. All the men from my relationships seemed nice enough. I mean, I was treated pretty well, at first, and I thought they loved me. Then, I took a deep breath and dug really deep, down to the space where none of us likes to go, to the place where we think only our demons live. I knew I had to. I wanted answers, so that I could have better relationships and love myself again. I took a long hard look in the mirror of my soul and reviewed the final stages of all my past relationships.

What I saw was that, in each relationship, I had either become physically ill, emotionally vulnerable, or just not my happy self and that changed the way these men looked at me and maybe even felt about me. I remembered how I ignored the first uneasy feeling that surfaced in all my relationships and, over the years, how I continued to ignore the countless uneasy feelings that kept creeping in. The sleepless nights while they were 'out with friends,' the secret telephone calls, the suspicious behavior, and the way I was blamed for being too sensitive or exaggerating events as I spoke up and said what I was truly feeling. As I started listening more to myself and acknowledging that things weren't as I thought they would be, I remembered seeing even bigger changes in the way I was treated.

There were countless signs and yet what story was I telling myself as to why all of this was acceptable? Did I really believe he still loved me? Was it alright to continue to feel like this, to be treated this way, and why had I kept ignoring my true gut feelings?

Somewhere in the depths of my soul there had to be a part of me that wanted to stop ignoring myself, because what happened next was the beginning of the end.

With my eyes starting to open to the truths in front of me and after years of dealing with addictive personalities, I decided it was time to take action. Once again, as I had in past relationships, I confronted the person I was with and once again, I received the same reaction and then felt the same way: he said it was all my fault, I was the one overreacting. I was making things up, there was nothing wrong, and it was all just me.

My heart broke into a million pieces.

I had no option but to face the truth: I was in another bad relationship. My life was crumbling underneath me. I wondered if I would ever recover. All I knew was that I had to make some hard choices.

So, there I was, after Day One of this three-day event, reliving my life. Only this time, I thought about it as if I was telling someone a story. Wow, the realization hit me of how strong and immensely intense this story was, that I actually believed my heart would be broken forever.

"You have permission to walk away from anything that doesn't feel right. Trust your instincts and listen to your inner-voice – it's trying to protect you." ~ **Bryant McGill**

The End and The Beginning

It wasn't easy for me to truly accept that my dream was over of having a great relationship and the kind of love that lasts forever. My heart was shattered, my world was shaken to the very core, and I spiraled into what felt like a living coma. I could barely function.

Thank God for my son and being able to see him every other week which helped me to pretend that I was okay and that everything was going to be alright.

As I prepared on the morning of Day Two, my thoughts about my story were stronger than ever, along with the memory of the demeaning and controlling behavior I had subjected myself to. I desperately wanted this event to change my life immediately! I so wanted the instructor to tell me what the trick was, to give me the magic pill, or tell me which door to choose to get out of this twisted story and just be happy again. I was at my wit's end and even wondered, *Is it possible to kill myself by jumping out of my two-storey apartment window?* Luckily, my sarcastic sense of humor kicked in and I figured I'd probably only break an arm or a leg. Plus, really, I didn't want to leave my son or die.

As I was about to leave, my mother called, doing her best to support me, and said, "God only gives us those challenges that we can handle." I had to laugh and thought God must be crazy and or this was His version of a really cruel joke. While I was driving to the event, I really wanted to curl up like an armadillo and hide. I could barely muster up a positive thought about myself, let alone comprehend the amount of inner strength, courage, and confidence that was about to emerge from deep within me.

"There will come a time when you believe everything is finished. That will be the beginning." ~ **Unknown Author**

Awakened: Welcome Back!

I was told that on Day Two everyone feels the same and no one really wants to go back. Something inside me said, *Lynn, you have a choice. Do you want to continue feeling like you do now, or do you want to have your life back?* I have to assume I was committed to seeing this weekend event through because I swallowed hard, took a deep breath, remembered how strong I was, and walked through the doors of the building. I sat in the same seat except now I had a few familiar faces around me. Although I felt more at ease, little did I know I was about to embark on another day in the amazing journey that would help to save my life! Thoughts of my mother's words came to mind. My mother was great at life philosophies, so I took what she said to heart. Having no clue of what to expect, I *now* stood, *powerfully determined to change my life and so it did!*

As I listened intently, the speaker proposed the following: **We are not our stories. It's 'just what happened.' It is what we chose to believe, think, and feel about that story that we hold on to and are attached to, that alters our lives, choices, and actions.**

The haze was lifting and it all started making sense to me. If I viewed my relationships as a story, then what had I been telling myself, and what was I choosing to believe about me? The concept that we create our own stories was one of the most powerful things I learned while attending this event. In fact, I still believe in the power of our stories to this day.

In Day Two of this magnificent and powerful life-altering three-day event, we shattered the illusion of our stories. We got down to the heart of what we tell ourselves: we were able to change not only the past and how we see it, we *learned to create and stand in the truth of our new future.*

It was now Day Three of the event. As I left the parking lot, there was a little bounce of confidence in my step and my whole body felt lighter. In making my way through the double doors to the auditorium, my heart, soul, and face were beaming with joy! All the fake Everything's Great smiles we had worn on Day One were now genuine grins of delight as we all hugged, acknowledging each other's triumphs! My body could genuinely feel a shift, a change, a sense of peace, as if a part of me was reawakening. There had always been a part of me that believed life was meant to be lived In Joy. It was as if a part of me knew there was more to life than the elaborate tale of woe, lies, and deceit that I had made up, believed in, and had once chosen to live. Now I was choosing to no longer accept the words, actions, or choices from all my past relationships as the truth. With my feet firmly planted and joy in my heart, I stood strong, passionately believing in myself again. It was time to take my power back, listen to my inner voice, and trust what I knew to be true!

Although I may not remember exactly what else was said in those three days, I know that the faith my mother raised me with, my own sense of knowing, my belief in something greater than myself, and my belief in the spiritual realm, helped to renew my soul. It felt as if the sun's brilliance was shining on a cloudy day. My eyes twinkled with confidence. I felt better prepared to make choices, to have a great life. The very depth of my being had been awakened to who I really am, and I knew that life is definitely worth living!

On Sunday, Day Three of the event, there was no fear or apprehension. All of us were eager now to make our way through the parking lot and into the building. It was as if everyone felt the energy had shifted and couldn't help but smile. The huge hugs we gave each other were our way of acknowledging and honoring the enlightening journey we had all just been through. A pure sense of joy and love filled the auditorium that night! I knew then I was going to be alright and everything was right with my world. I left there that night trusting once again in love, magic, miracles, and me!

There Are No Coincidences

When I left the event, I decided to celebrate my new Awakened state by buying myself dinner. When I got up to pay, the server told me that the person ahead of me had paid for my meal.

I was in shock. Nothing like that had ever happened to me in my entire life! Why had that person been so gracious to me? Why then, at that precise moment in time when I felt such a sense of renewal, of love, so alive as if awakened back to believing and trusting in myself and something greater again? Why then?

In contemplating that we are the creators of our stories, the awareness fell over me like a soft gentle breeze: I was the one responsible for the story I told myself. I finally realized that I had chosen to create these stories about *all* my relationships. It was these stories that would bring me to the point of questioning myself in order to realize that I can truly trust my quiet inner voice. Feeling my power return, I knew it was now time to let go, to forgive myself and all the men I had chosen who taught me, in this moment, how to love myself again.

Well, I'd like to believe from the chills and tears I get as I type this (I have to believe it is true), it was my quiet inner voice whispering, *Welcome Back!*

CHAPTER 13

REBIRTH

Samantha Bishop

Not again. This can't be happening again. The voice inside my head is desperate and pleading. The lights inside the bedroom are giving off a soft golden glow as twilight approaches.

Can't I at least be on the soft warm bed instead of stuck on this freezing cold tile?! My mind won't shut off even as my body is shutting down.

There is a pain tearing through my abdomen like a searing hot knife and my lungs can only take in wisps of air. I am very slowly losing consciousness as I lay quietly gasping for breath on the bathroom floor.

My husband is just fifteen feet away on the bed, but he can't see me from where he is. *I need help. I should make a noise.* My mind is trying to make plan, trying to survive, but I don't move.

A deeper part of me doesn't want him to find me, yet again. To see the hysterical fear etched upon his face. To know that he will call an ambulance. Doctors, nurses, specialist, tests and no conclusions.

"Yes, Mrs. Nuhfer, you are definitely sick. We just have no idea what is causing all of these symptoms. We'll continue testing until we find the cause."

I don't want to be found. This time I just want to fade away. I'm not feeling fear. In fact, beyond the pain, it feels like I'm floating. I just want to float and drift like dandelion fluff on the breeze. No more trying. No more exhaustion, frustration, and pain, but he knows something's wrong. He hasn't heard me moving for a while and he comes to find me.

Here we go again. He's on the phone with 911. Through half open eyes, I can see him on the phone. He's pacing and frantic while he talks to the 911 operator. In that moment, I love him and simultaneously want to get as far away from him as I can. In fact, I want to get away from everything.

I've been sick, stuck and unchanging for far too many years. Married at 22, graduate school at 24, thyroid cancer at 26, complete hysterectomy at 30, gallbladder removed at 31, and now at 41 here I am. I'm on the floor of my bathroom, in excruciating pain, losing consciousness.

It's hard for me to say that I have had a bad life up to this point; I have had my struggles: A physically, mentally, and emotionally abusive father. Almost daily sexual abuse from age four to age twelve from a family member and also from a church elder. As soon as I could get away, I ran to college and then ran into the arms of a safe and loving man. I sought safety and control in everything I did. In the outside world I was safe. In retrospect, too safe. On the inside, inside of my body, I was anything but safe and in control. The Universe was attempting to get my attention again, and as I ignored every sign, they just kept coming in the form of illness.

This time, this sign, I was no longer going to ignore. This time I needed to look deeper, to go inside and stare my truth in the eyes. I was scared to death, but I was ready. Something had to change. Safety, security, and control: these things weren't bringing me fulfillment, joy, and vibrant health. But where to start....

A year prior to finding myself on the floor of my bathroom gasping for breath, I was yet again looking for a change. To outside eyes I had a great life. A decent marriage, academic success, a beautiful home, and successful self-employment. Yet, I was empty, unfulfilled and seeking to fill a growing void that seemed vast and endless. I changed my hair, my clothes, my home decor. I changed careers, got more degrees, learned to play the violin. Nothing filled that ever-growing void.

For years, I spent nights and sometimes days, in secret, crying to the Universe, *Please show me exactly what I am meant to do. Show me my path. I'm ready. I'll do anything as long as it fills me and serves a greater purpose!* I begged and begged like a broken record. I knew there was more, I just didn't know what.

Having dealt with poor health for years, I decided that maybe a drastic change in my diet would solve my problems and give me clarity. I remembered hearing about a new documentary about juice fasting called "Fat Sick and Nearly Dead." I was already a vegetarian, and had been toying with the idea of going one hundred percent raw vegan. I had diligently done my research, and decided that a sixty-day juice fast was the perfect way to detox, reset my taste buds and transition into an all raw vegan diet.

I had read stories of people doing this and having their lives completely change. Not only would they detox from old food habits, but they would emotionally detox as well. Old ways of life and relationships would no longer feel right and would fall away. That all sounded amazing, but I really had no idea what I was about to experience.

Thirty days into the fast, I'm sitting in yoga class meditating. "Take a deep breath in through your nose, and on the exhale let your awareness fall deep behind your belly button," the yoga instructor offered. I remember feeling the old wooden floor beneath my folded legs. The room was overly warm do to the age of the building and an extremely hot and humid Ohio summer day. A trickle of sweat is tickling from the base of my head down my comfortably erect spine. I haven't had solid food in thirty days, and I feel light as air. Not tired. Not weak. Just light. My mind is free and untroubled without the normal chatter and images that reside there. I am alive with awareness and it feels as though my cells are lightly vibrating. I am noticing that the woman next to me is wearing a lemon scented fragrance, and with the humidity in the room I can taste its tartness on my tongue. There is no airflow in the room, but I swear I can feel a breeze caressing my skin like cool silk. My senses are so alive. The experience of shutting down the digestive process while juice fasting has opened up a sensory world I never knew. It was a complete high.

I breathed deeply through my nose as guided, and on the exhale WHOOSH! I was out of my body and twenty times my physical size. I was the size of the room. I was everywhere and everything at once. A calm washed over me. That empty void was gone. Contentment filled my awareness and wholeness was my reality. It must have only taken seconds, and with the instructor's next words I was back inside my body. All I could think in that moment was, *I want more of that! Please show me how to live there.* It would take a very long time and dramatic changes before I would know that wholeness again.

As the fast progressed, I knew it was time to get off all of the medications I had been on for the past twelve years. Fibromyalgia, hypothyroidism, and migraines came with a toxic medicine cabinet: muscle relaxers, pills for nerve pain, all around pain killers, and the occasional anti-anxiety medications. If I was really going to detox my body and my life, the medications had to go. I quit cold turkey without the help of the doctors who had prescribed them or the knowledge of my husband. While I don't recommend this, and I knew that I would be advised not to, I was ready to be free.

My days and nights were spent in pain, sleepless and exhausted. My body had come to rely on the medications for sleep and pain relief. I wasn't eating. I was juicing so there was nothing to help numb the sensations. Many times, I found myself on the floor of my office, heart racing, thoughts swirling, cold sweat soaking through my clothes. I felt like I needed to jump out of my skin and run away. Panic attacks! Detoxing was a wild ride. Food had always been my favorite way to numb. Now all I had was juice, pain, and my reality. No medications to numb the physical pain. No food to stuff down and shut out the reality that my life was rapidly changing, and I didn't like what I saw.

I saw a marriage without intimacy and never being truly seen by my partner. A business that devoured my time, my thoughts and my energy. A family that valued hard work and sacrifice over happiness and self-care. I saw myself trying to please everyone at all times and mold my life around these realities. It was no longer working.

I guess I thought the juice fast would fix everything. Fix all of these problems somehow magically. It gave me something to concentrate on. Another distraction. Getting physically healthy would be the key. I didn't realize that my emotional unhealthiness was fueling the physical symptoms. Juicing put that beautifully yet painfully into sharp focus.

After the juice fast was complete, my life as a raw vegan began. I loved eating raw, whole, alive fruits and vegetables. I had energy and my body looked amazing. After a life with no thyroid, no ovaries, and no gallbladder, that was a reality I thought I would never experience again. I was healthier than I had been in fifteen years. Where was the contentment? The fulfillment? The wholeness? Why was I experiencing "new" illnesses that were a complete mystery to the doctors? My tests said that I was the picture of health. I looked like the picture of health, and yet.......

I'm on the floor of my bathroom at 41-years-old gasping for breath and wishing I could just fade away.

I'm not happy. That's now obvious. I feel completely lost in my own life. There has to be more. I felt wholeness and contentment that day in meditation. I know it exists. That was the mantra running in my head twenty-four hours a day. I was a married woman, a business owner, and my support community was small and conservative. If I was to believe what my family always said, my happiness didn't matter. My need for wholeness didn't matter. I had responsibilities and commitments. Besides, what would everyone think and say?

My life needed to change and there was no turning back. I needed freedom. I needed to explore who I was at my core. My inside was changing, my awareness and consciousness was changing. I had never stepped into my life and looked at who I really was. Juicing helped me to do this, but now what? I could see that I had always chosen safety and security over fulfillment and happiness. I chose everyone else's story of who I should be. In the small rural town where I grew up, marriage was the expectation for women. My father took it one step further. My parents weren't in a loving relationship. There was no affection, only passable tolerance. My father stayed out of commitment and responsibility and my mother stayed to be taken care of. One day when I was eighteen, my father and I were running an errand together. I had been dating the same boy for two years, and I was about to graduate high school. To my father, that was when a woman was supposed to find a man and start a family. As we drove he started talking.

"I know you have been dating this boy for a while now. You have to be thinking about whether he can be a good provider. Love has nothing to do with it. A woman should never look for love. She should look for a man who can take care of her, keep her safe, and provide."

"Dad, I want to find a man I can be happy with. I can provide for myself."

"That is a selfish attitude. A woman's place is in the home caring for her husband and her children. You won't be able to provide when you have babies, and you'll need a reliable man who can provide for you and your children. Your mother and I aren't in love. I wanted a family and I stay to provide for all of you. Your mother stays because she knows that is her place and she will be provided for."

I was appalled by this. I would have my career and love! Yet, safety and security is what I ran toward. Even as I fought his words, they still steered my life. Now I had what I was supposed to have, married to a safe provider, career, home owner. Yet, I wasn't fully alive. It was a half-life, cocooned away from fear and risk, lost and shoved into a box of societal convention.

The most confronting change that needed to occur was my marriage. It was the box of safety and conformity I lived in, but it came at far too high a price. Namely, my rapidly dying sensual side. Sex and intimacy was never a big part of our marriage, but through the years of school, careers, and sickness it had faded to nothing. I tried. I really tried. I needed the connection that intimacy brought, so I tried. I craved the aliveness that sexual contact stirred within me. I constantly came up with ideas to spice things up. I saw something on a talk show once about how thirty days of sex every day, no excuses, could revive the intimacy in a marriage. I begged him to give it a shot. He agreed begrudgingly. We lasted three days. Still, I had to try. Our relationship felt like that of roommates, and sometimes worse, that of parent and child. *God, I just want to be touched, to be seen, to be desired.* I was starting to see how the lack of this had been starving me, shriveling and shrinking that sensual woman inside of me. That vital passionate energy was fading.

One more effort, I said to myself. I was sitting on our king-sized bed one hot summer afternoon. My husband was on the sofa in the living room. He was working on his laptop, his cell phone beside him updating him on the score of a baseball game in progress, and the television in front of him was playing a different baseball game. This was typical of our limited time together. We weren't actually engaging each other and yet, he wanted me home and close by, just to know I was there. That was all the intimacy he needed. To have me close by.

One more effort. I sat there on the bed achingly lonely, longing to be seen, touched, acknowledged. I stood up and slowly undressed. I was feeling good in my skin. The juice fast had my body feeling alive and energized, the need for connection was burning just under my skin. *I have to try this with him again....*

As I slid the clothes from my body, the warm, soft breeze wafted like silk across my skin. The heat of the day mixing with the warm breeze made my body and my senses feel like they were melting into the air around me, becoming one with everything at once. It felt so sensual. I wanted my partner, the man in my life, to join me in this experience. I hesitated. Words I had heard him say before came back to me now as I stood there in this moment of desire.

"I don't know why. I just don't care for sex," he would say apologetically and a little apathetically.

Still, one more effort....

I walked slowly from the bedroom, feeling vulnerable, sensual, and full of longing until I was standing before him. I was nervous, but empowered standing there owning my naked desire. What seemed like an eternity passed with no acknowledgment. *I know he sees me!* Finally, without looking up, he spoke. His only words,

"Very funny."

Very funny???!!! My need for intimacy? My attempt at connection? My naked body? What was funny?! I said nothing. I had no words. What could be said? This was my marriage. This was my life. My heart raced and my emotions flashed between embarrassment, frustration, and resignation. The empowered sensual woman ducked down in my soul and disappeared once again. I wanted to run and not stop. I walked quickly back to our bedroom and dressed in humiliation. I sat back down on the bed in anguish. *I could be married to this man for another fifty years. No intimacy. Not being seen. This will be my reality!*

Flashes of memories poured in as I sat there. The time we went out to eat with friends, and I tried a sip of my friend's beer. It was a Blue Moon, citrusy with orange slices in it. It tasted like warm liquid bread. I loved it and ordered one of my own. I didn't realize that I liked beer until that moment. It was exciting. Something new. I loved new experiences! My husband was noticeably disapproving and silent toward me the rest of the evening. When we got home, I asked what was bothering him.

He said with disappointment in his voice, "I can't believe you ordered a beer! We don't drink beer! We aren't THOSE people!"

Those people? I was a person who loved new experiences, and open-mindedness. That is the kind of person I am. Still, I had been shamed, and I never order a beer again.

Or recently, when my girlfriend invited me to a "Pure Romance" party for women. It was a party where women could get together and discreetly check out intimate toys for herself or for sharing with her partner. It was new and sounded fun. I never got out with friends, and spending time with women sounded like a good thing. I hadn't yet decided whether I was going to go. Then my husband found the information pamphlet and with complete disgust said, "You aren't even considering this, are you?!"

The way he looked at me brought up such shame, I couldn't even look him in the eye. Now as I sat here on the edge of the bed, rejected and alone, those memories just brought up anger and complete clarity. These and so many other signs were urging me to reclaim my life.

I have to leave my marriage! I can't grow and flourish here. If I stay, part of me will surely die. This was the new mantra in my head. Waves of fear and emotion would crash over me day and night. *How? When? How? How? How?!!!*

Now don't get me wrong here. I do not lay the blame of the unhappiness of my marriage at the feet of my husband. That couldn't be further from the truth. I feel culpable. Equal or greater culpability, to be exact. All he ever wanted was for me to stay exactly as I was when he married me, to be that same 22-year-old self, but I didn't. I couldn't. That need for change and growth on my own terms in a stagnant environment made me unhappy, not just the lack of intimacy and the many other ways a couple can be discordant. He would have stayed with me for the rest of our lives, loving me. On his terms of course, but faithful and loving just the same. I didn't know who I was when I met him, because my father had dictated who everyone in his household should be. I was destined to change and grow. I had to in order to feel alive. It was now time to find out just who I could be. Who I needed to be.

Emotionally, I knew I could not count on my family to support the leaving of my marriage. They loved my husband as one of the family. He was a great provider. They believed in self-sacrifice and martyrdom. Growing up I never saw my mother or father engage in self-care. They led hard lives of sacrifice. Working in factories and raising a family of six with very little money. They didn't live their dreams. In fact, I'm not sure they even remember what their dreams were. They were truly miserable in their marriage, but they reminded us daily that they stayed together for us children. Life was about sucking it up. My father was fond of saying,

"Life is hard. It isn't about being happy, it is about surviving and getting by. All of those people out there 'searching for happiness' is what is wrong with this world. Keep your head down and work hard. Be a good person, and you can rest in heaven when you die."

My family will not support this! They will do everything they can to tell me why it is wrong for me to leave. When my sister came out of the closet, they didn't support her. They cut her out of their lives and didn't look back. They embraced her ex-husband as their new son, and acted as if she never existed. I was scared and desperate but determined. I needed to distance myself from those who would try to keep me where I was due to their own fears and beliefs. I needed to leave and start over somewhere else. It may not have been completely rational, but it was my reality at that time.

My mind was full of relentless chatter day and night, night and day. *You have to listen this time. Your unhappiness is making you sick.* I went to yoga seven days a week, and three days a week, I went twice a day. The yoga mat was the only place I found peace and a quiet mind. It was my anchor in the storm, and it also gave me strength to choose my well-being over all else. It taught me that until I experienced my own well-being, I could not be effective at being a positive influence in this world. *I want to make a difference. I want to be of service in the world,* my mind whispered during meditation. This is my path. A path of service. I have my answer. *Okay, but what does that mean? What does that look like? I'm so lost.*

I knew that in distancing myself and starting over I needed to leave my business, my bakery. I loved and resented my business equally. It gave me purpose yet it was a weight, an anchor. The bakery was open six days a week, but I worked seven. I got to work between 5 a.m. and 6 a.m. depending upon how many pre-orders they were to bake for the day, and I wouldn't come home until around 7 or 8 p.m. I had an assistant baker, but I did 85 per cent of the baking. It was constant baking, shopping, cleaning, paperwork, employee management, customer relations, inventory management and product development. The bakery was in a historic building built in 1860, so the wiring, plumbing, heating and cooling systems were forever breaking down. It was all a great distraction, and an excuse to be away from home. It was something else to throw myself into in order not to look at the emptiness I felt. It had also been an effective way to numb. So much delicious sugar, my favorite drug. The juice fast had made it almost painful to be at the bakery. The scent of baked goods was torture. Now with my addiction to sugar broken, and the crutch of numbing with food gone, I could see the bakery for the role it played in my life. I could also see how exhausted I was. It was time to let it go.

I was ready to leave, but where was I going? I didn't have many friends. I had immersed myself in my marriage and my work over those 20 years. Without my husband, my family, my business or the support of friends, I had nothing keeping me in Ohio. I wanted to go away some place that was as different as I felt. Some place that felt as new and different as I was becoming.

I had been to California only once. I had never had the desire to go there. Earthquakes scared me, and my parents had always blamed the world's problems on 'the type of people who live in California.' In fact, my father had been heard many times to say that we would be better off if "California just fell into the ocean."

So, when I finally ended up visiting California a couple of years before, I was shocked to find myself in love. My husband and I had visited Big Sur on a week-long vacation. It was nothing like I expected. I remember standing on the beach mesmerized. I had never seen the Pacific Ocean. It held me transfixed by its beauty and its energy. With hypothyroidism, I really don't like being damp and cold. As I stood on that chilly windswept beach with the waves crashing in, I felt more at peace and at home and relaxed in my body than I had ever felt in Ohio. The smell of salt and the pounding waves called to me, refreshed my soul, and soothed a deep ache like a balm. Now California was calling me back there.

I knew someone from my past who lived in California. I hadn't spoken to this friend in over 20 years, but something inside encouraged me to reach out. It was out of character for me to reach out to someone like this, but then everything in my life seemed out of character lately. The only thing I could do was follow my intuition, and my intuition was calling me to California. The minute I reached out to my friend, a ball started rolling that went faster than I ever anticipated. My friend was excited to hear from me. His mother had passed away and left him a condo that was falling into disrepair. He didn't want to sell the condo and couldn't bring himself to spend any time there due to painful memories. I could live there for free if I spent my time cleaning, fixing it up and caring for it. It was in very rough shape, but it was free and would afford me a fresh start.

I now had a destination for my new life. It fit the bill. Now, I had no excuses. It was time to say goodbye.

I was sitting at my computer at work. My heart was pounding so hard, I swear they can hear it in the kitchen downstairs. I see spots swimming before my eyes, and yet I experience a deep stillness: I know that my husband feels this coming, and I decide to write him a letter. We are both too emotional for words. I had tried words and he would shut me down. Tried to tell him what was happening in my soul. I approached him many times to talk. He won't let me in. He walks away. So, I write, and I write. I try my best to explain what has been happening inside of me. He has been along for the roller coaster ride of my health. He has witnessed my desperate numbing through food and shopping, the constant change of careers and more schooling, he knows my bleak unhappiness, our disconnection and lack of intimacy, but I write it all out.

If I am going to be sick, at least I am going to be happy.

My heart is breaking, but in the breaking a space is already opening. A quiet shift is happening as I pour my heart on the page. My first plea for my own inner need.

"I can't do this anymore. I love you, and I will always love you, but I am dying inside. I went from my father's home to your home with no time to decide or discover who I really am or what I really want in my life. I am so so sorry…."

Dusk was approaching and the stillness was palpable. I can smell freshly baked chocolate cake wafting up the stairs to my office. I do love this bakery, but it is equal parts too much and not enough. It isn't me anymore. I can hear a woman laughing downstairs as she buys baked goodies to take home to her family. It seems everything is normal and life is continuing forward for everyone else as my hands shake and tears fall hot and wet onto the keyboard. My hand hovers over the send button. Once I send this, there is no turning back. I won't let myself, I can't let myself turn back. This moment will change my life forever. "I AM LEAVING. I NEED TO BE FREE. I NEED MORE." I feel a deeply supportive presence hovering invisible in the room. I feel a knowing that this is right. I press send…. here I go.

It is all a fog now, like I was being moved though my days guided by that invisible hand. Tears and fights, love and resentment being jumbled together in every moment. Life was a mix of pain and exhilaration. One moment I would find myself at 3 a.m. sitting in my car in the parking lot at the end of the street sobbing uncontrollably. Another fight. A police officer pulls up and is flashing his flashlight in on me. He knocks on the window. He wants to know why I am here sobbing at 3 a.m.

"Is your husband violent, ma'am? Are you afraid to go home? Do you have a place to stay tonight?" the officer inquires dutifully.

Through broken sobs I actually laugh. "No, he's a pacifist. We are just going through separation and it's hard. Hard for both of us."

Then I would swing to moments of utter elation and euphoria. *I'm free! My life, my world is opening up! I have choices! It's really happening!*

I had no play book, no role model or instructions for what I was doing. I was on autopilot, packing, arranging, organizing. It was as if something deep within me knew what to do, and I was along for the ride. What was I to bring with me? The art that I loved? Furniture I collected and refinished? Photo albums that had 20 plus years of memories. No. As I stood frozen in my kitchen facing a house full of memories, I decided it would be a completely fresh start. Everything I touched had an energetic attachment to the past. A connection to a life with which I no longer resonated. I picked up one of the gorgeous hand-blown glasses I drank juice out of every morning. Swirls of soft blue, sea-foam green, pearly white and violet. I loved those glasses, each unique and hand-picked, but now they were just ties to memories. They wouldn't be coming with me. I wanted nothing, I needed nothing. I packed up a quarter of my wardrobe and some important kitchen equipment. That is all I would bring. I was ready for everything to change.

If I thought telling him I was leaving was going to be difficult, I had no idea how difficult it would be to leave and start over.

The years following the separation and then divorce were a mêlée of self-doubt, deep knowingness, and sharp loneliness. I had no job having left my business behind. I was 3000 miles from my home, my family, comfort, familiarity and the man who had been my constant companion my entire adult life.

I had taken on the cleaning and renovating of my friend's run-down condo in exchange for a place to live. That kept my days full, but it was total isolation. I knew one person and that person was busy and in their own world most of the time. *WHAT HAVE I DONE!? Should I go back to my old life? Was sleepwalking and numbing out better than this isolation and pain?*

Still, I was free, starting over, taking risks, and changing. I was changing every day. The changes were scary but necessary. I was seeing more of the real me, and I was very lost and insecure. I had no idea how I had been someone's partner for 23 years. I didn't even know how to be with myself. The freedom came with the reality of mountains of self-work. Digging myself out of the hole of false security and into the light of my own inner worth and power.

As the days went by, I started to let go of my home so far away. A part of me was fighting the newness, fighting the stark differences, and making it harder for myself than it had to be. Many people in Los Angeles are transplants, and a lovely acquaintance gave me some good advice to get me past my resistance. I had gone to a yoga class and struck up a conversation with a man from Australia. Going to yoga had been my refuge back home, and I just couldn't find a yoga studio that felt like home to me in LA. I felt like the one thing that kept me calm, centered and able to cope was being taken away. This feeling had me particularly sad and irritated at the yoga studio that day. As I stood there feeling lost yet again, like an island, a woman without a home, this kind Australian man said hello.

"Hello," I muttered back, but I immediately looked down at my feet hoping the conversation wouldn't go any further. I didn't feel comfortable at this new studio and I was contemplating leaving before class started, but he persisted, picking up his mat and moving closer to me so that we could talk. He was kind with warm brown eyes and a pleasant smile. From the accent, I knew he was Australian.

"I've never seen you here before. Are you new to the area?"

That was my opening, all I needed to launch into just how new I was here. I had found someone to reach out to, someone obviously not from here who could understand how unfamiliar, different and unfriendly this new place felt. The words rushed out of me like a torrent. I felt bad for dumping all over this gentle stranger, but I couldn't stop the words. This lovely yogi listened to my angst with beautiful patience and a knowing heart. He smiled and sighed deeply.

"I used to do what you are doing, but you have to stop comparing where you came from to where you are. They both have their assets and deficiencies. If you are always comparing, you can't be present and enjoy where you are."

He placed his hand lightly on my back as we walked into class whispering in a low voice that washed over me like a balm,

"Be present and concentrate on the assets. There are many all around you."

He had heard me, really heard me. He could relate, yet he was no longer suffering as I was.

All through the asanas that day his words hummed in my ears. I started to let my new home, my new city into my heart rather than keeping her at arm's length. With each breath and each movement of my body, I started to sink into my new life at last. I invited it in, asking it to be gentle with me and embrace me. I was allowing myself to be here and be present for the first time since the move, maybe for the first time in my life. I never went back to that studio, so I never saw that wise yogi again. Was he an angel, a messenger sent to settle my heart? Maybe. Whether he was or not, his words gave me my home back, and I will forever be grateful.

The years since have brought epiphanies, new experiences, constant self-work and growth, and a life path that I could have never dreamed possible. I am now so at peace and at home that my previous life feels like a dream, like a story of someone else's life about which I once read. The biggest most beautiful awakening has been the full awareness that home is within me. I am never without my home and it can never be taken away. I am home in my body and in my soul, entirely free. I am worth the risks I took to get here. Worth every moment of effort to come home to myself and find my path in this world.

Am I complete? Is the awakening process finally over? No. I don't think it ever will be. As I walk through life, I go deeper and deeper still. I am forever peeling back the layers of who I am and what my path of service will look like in this world. I meet each day with the knowledge that when I was faced with my awakening, I stepped into it. I didn't turn away and choose to sleep. I embraced it, stepped on the wave of the Universe and took the ride. I was tumbled on the rocks, held down, and dragged along the rough and sandy bottom, but I also got to ride the wave. I think I'll continue to ride that wave with the rocks and undertow, fully awake, alive and at home.

CHAPTER 14

SELF-LOVE

Caroline Smith

One of the things I remember most clearly from that night is the sight of the crimson red, blood-stained water. After coming home to what I thought was an empty house, I heard water rushing and went to examine what I thought was a plumbing malfunction. Instead I found a bathtub full of blood, thick as syrup, red as a ruby. It was like a scene out of an episode of *Dexter*. My husband was sitting in the water, with glassy eyes, a faraway look on his face, and a kitchen knife in his hand.

I gasped, jumped back from the tub, and tried to close the shower curtain, only to have the entire shower rod collapse to the ground. I couldn't escape the gore, the pervasive *redness*, the excessive amount of blood. That scarlet, bloody image would invade my psyche for the next year every time I saw a glass of Merlot, a singing cardinal, or a bowl of fresh strawberries.

"What did you do? What did you do?" I repeatedly begged of him.

"I've come to peace with everything. This is what I want. I'm ready to be done," he responded.

I remember thinking to myself with the blotchy, scrunched-up face that usually accompanies an ugly cry, *Why am I not crying right now? Where are all of my tears?!* Looking back, I realize that I must've been in shock: in shock from the sound of water running randomly after a couple of hours of peaceful, silent solitude in a home that had recently become vocally-violent, emotionally-charged, and completely chaotic; in shock from the smell of my own fear when I realized what I was witnessing; in shock from the overwhelming feeling of defeat emanating from his dark brown eyes.

It was like nothing I'd ever experienced before and nothing I ever hope to experience again. It was a night so full of emotion, a night witnessing and walking the fine line between life and death, and *the* night that made me realize I'd reached a turning point in my own personal journey. I knew my story was about to change dramatically, and that my life would never again look the same.

After eight years together, countless amazing memories, and a few bad months, we were moving in two completely different directions. Without consciously realizing it, my expectations of the kind of relationship I wanted to be in had evolved. He no longer fit the image of the kind of partner I wanted, and he wasn't willing to take personal responsibility for his own happiness. A few days earlier we'd decided to call it quits. We'd agreed to end things civilly and respect each other throughout the process. But now all rules were out the window.

Bath time used to be my ME time, my meditation. I had bubbles, salts, essential oils, and candles. My bath was when I washed my stress away, soaked in life's lessons, reflected on my day, quieted voices in my head, and allowed myself to just be. I remember thinking that on top of all the guilt, the shame, and the pain of our impending divorce, he'd taken my bath time from me. Of all the places and ways he could've chosen to try to end his life, he picked my favorite place in the house (and one of my favorite places in the world). I would never look at a bathtub the same and thought I would never again carelessly soak in the comfort of steaming water.

Ugh, how selfish it felt to even think about myself when he was clearly in so much pain that he was willing to try to take his own life. But deep down inside, there was a voice telling me: *No matter what was happening with him, no matter how much I loved him, it was time to live life for* **me**, *to put myself first and truly love myself above anyone else.* The voice was telling me that it was okay to think those selfish thoughts, to be honest about how I felt in this terrifying moment, to put myself first. The voice helped me figure out that what had been missing from our relationship, and what ultimately led to its demise, was my own self-love.

It took me a full 18 months to take a bath again, to allow myself that soothing indulgence, to experience joy and pleasure in the same setting that was the source of my PTSD and the near-end of an incredible soul. Every time I went to fill the tub (and it didn't matter where I was – my new apartment, my parents' house, a hotel), all I could think about was finding him floating there, giving up on life. I had so many emotions that made me feel like shit and the only thing I wanted to do was soak them away in a steaming bath, but I just couldn't bring myself to do it.

Throughout the next year and a half, I slowly learned to love myself again without the refuge of my cherished bath time. Through tear-soaked therapy sessions and yoga classes spent lying on the ground sobbing, through phone calls and conversations with friends and family who didn't understand how everything went so badly so quickly, I realized that I was experiencing an awakening - a painful, raw, emotional awakening.

I remember one specific call with my dad while I was going through the separation, when he asked me, "Are you sure you're not taking the easy way out? Do you think you can still love him and make it work?"

All I could do was break down into tears and between sobs tell him, "I do still love him, but I need to love myself more. This is far from easy. Easy would be staying and pretending everything is still okay."

Some days it felt like the only thing keeping me going was some inherent knowledge of a richer, fuller, more authentic life I would be living when I finally made it to the other side. I had big plans and even bigger dreams. Now there was no one else to consider, no barriers except the ones I placed on myself.

I had lost myself along the way during those eight years of marriage. I had buried my own love in the idea that the unconditional love of another was love's truest form. And while my beloved bath time was one piece of self-love I *had* been practicing, it was superficial and incomplete. Without the distraction of bath time and through the 20-20 lens of hindsight, I slowly realized that a lot of my personal habits were the same. I could lead a full class to a place of acceptance and peace through movement, meditation, and presence, but I couldn't quite find that same acceptance and peace for myself. I could give friends the best advice, but I never took my own advice. I could fight for the needs of my loved ones, but I never fought for my own needs as Number One. A flicker of self-love kept me going: months of personal work and many, many hours of nurturing and true self-care blossomed into the beautiful life I now enjoy.

I'll back it up a bit. I've always been a helper. My mom's favorite way to get me to do something as a kid was to say, "Caroline, could you be so helpful and get me *whatever* from *wherever*?" Or, "Thank you, you're such a good helper."

Rather than striving to be the most beautiful or the smartest like my friends dreamed about, my life goals and values revolved around being the most helpful. For years, I wanted to be a doctor to help others heal. After taking pre-med courses and the MCAT in college, I realized I was more interested in people than science and switched my major to sociology. I got a Master's in public health, helped businesses get health insurance access for their employees, worked in corporate wellness helping companies get healthier, and finally found yoga (and the start of a *little* self-love) around the time that my relationship with my ex-husband got serious.

On our first real date together, he spilled his soul telling me that he felt so comfortable opening up to me. He told me of his past relationships, depression, goals, and dreams. I held his hand and listened, asked the right questions, and gave the right encouragement.

"My ex-girlfriend broke up with me because she said I was functionally depressed and not willing to change," he told me. "It took us breaking up for me to start going to the gym again, really focus on DJing, and do all the things that made me happy." I nodded in understanding, proud of his acceptance and growth from that break-up. Looking back on that conversation now feels like the creepy foreshadowing in a bad horror movie.

He was easy to love, a kind soul not unlike a puppy's, full of energy and passion, and maybe a bit lost. He needed me as the helper and lover I grew up and longed to be. I was the low-maintenance, cool girlfriend who was eager to please. I realize that I never fully opened up to him because I myself hadn't yet discovered and accepted the true me.

We moved cross-country together, got two dogs, had awesome friends, varied interests, and eventually got married. I quit my corporate job and started teaching yoga full time. I was playing the helper in my relationship, the helper in my career, and, on the surface, everything was great. We were the fun, easy-going couple who never fought. We did well in any social situation. We were both self-employed, chasing our dreams and living the life in Southern California. We were young and invincible. And then things changed.

I can now see the slow shifts, the subtle ways we drifted apart and grew in different directions, the pieces adding up to the whole. At the time, there was a day, even a moment, when things just felt different. I remember coming home after a long, tiring day of teaching to a messy house, with dogs who still hadn't been walked, and him playing video games and only looking up long enough to ask me, "What are we doing for dinner?"

It was then that I realized that my definition of a partner was different from his. I wanted more and needed *more*, even though it was hard to put into words what that was or how he wasn't fulfilling my needs. While that want and that need were directed at him, it took time to figure out that they were really about me. I wanted and desperately needed to be a different person, to FINALLY be true to myself, to be awake to my authentic being, and to love the real ME. I needed to learn how to put my feelings into words and requests and communicate those to my partner instead of expecting someone to read my mind.

At first our breakup was a little too easy. He sensed the distance between us over a weekend camping with friends and pulled away. I was annoyed with how he was acting. After a long day of hiking when I paid more attention to someone else than to him, he essentially threw a tantrum.

"Where did you go?" I asked him, after finishing the last mile of the hike practically running to try and catch up to him.

"You just walked away from me and I wanted to show you the waterfall, but I figured if you'd rather hang out with them, so I just finished the hike by myself," he responded.

The rest of the day didn't go much better. He sat in the car, demanding that we go home early and instead of communicating, we fought, one of the rare times we yelled and cried and sat in silent frustration before agreeing to try harder and start fresh.

After a few weeks, it was apparent that our fresh start wasn't working. We decided we shouldn't be together. We still wanted to be friends. We talked for hours and told each other, "It doesn't have to be like everyone else's breakups. I want you to be happy and if this is what you want then let's at least be friends."

And then, it wasn't easy. It was messy, bloody (literally), and more painful than I could've ever imagined. The symbolism of that night isn't lost on me. I remember the eerie silence, the quietness of the house. The dogs were eager for attention, as usual, but seemed somehow different, like they knew something I didn't know. I smoked a spliff, called a friend, explained he and I were splitting up, and just sat. I had spent the day away from town, in nature with someone who understood and accepted the "new," true me, and for a short moment I felt at peace and content despite the chaos of my married life unraveling. That's when I heard the water running in the bathtub.

When I tried calling 911, he held the knife to his throat, his eyes bulging, possessed with a fury I hadn't seen in the eight years we'd been together. I couldn't look in the tub; I couldn't witness the deep cuts he'd inflicted on himself. I screamed, I shook, but I still couldn't cry.

After what felt like hours but could've been minutes, we both realized he wasn't dying. I no longer wanted to play the helper. I wasn't going to plan a funeral for my young husband, but I wasn't going to be his nurse either. Because he refused to allow me to call an ambulance, I told him he had to get out of the tub and he had to wrap up his cuts and then we would figure out the next step.

"I can't help you right now, and I can't look at your cuts," I told him as

I threw him some bandanas and rags from the linen closet on the floor by the tub. "I'll be in the living room. If you can't take care of this yourself, I'm calling an ambulance." I marched out to the living room, retreating to neutral territory.

The old me would've helped him carefully wrap his legs, tending to him like a young child who fell off his bike. The new, awake me had to get the hell out of there. I couldn't be near his wounds - they represented all the things I couldn't help him with, things he had to deal with himself. As cruel as it sounds, I remember thinking, *He got himself into this. He can get himself out.* After wrapping his legs and draining the tub, he hobbled into the living room and we spent the night talking, calm and composed, before I drove him to the hospital the next morning.

Ultimately, he survived the flesh wounds. He survived 72 hours in the ER and psychiatric unit. He survived the months of us trying to make it work as friends before we cut communication and he moved away. The last communication we had, after months of not talking, was a pleasant email exchange where it was clear that he had more than survived – he's rebuilt his life and is thriving without me.

"I was in a really dark place when we split up. I've realized a lot of things since then," he wrote. "The other day I got yelled at by a big fashion photographer and just sat there calmly and took it. He had no idea how I remained so chill. But from all I've been through, I knew how unimportant that moment was. I wouldn't have been able to do that a couple of years ago."

We will both live with the scars of that night forever. Like tough scar tissue that rebuilds around a wound, we will never forget how we got where we are, and we are each stronger for what we've been through.

As tough as the night was when he tried to take his life, the months that followed challenged me more than my 31 years of life combined ever had.

Friendships that were once easy became strained, things that used to be important no longer mattered, and day-to-day existence felt pointless. Our relationship was a casualty of my own personal growth. While I wouldn't wish the experience on anyone, or want to go through it again, I know it had to happen to be where and who I am today. He later told me he was in a sort of trance when he cut myself, barely feeling the knife in his flesh, floating in and out of consciousness. There were many times I wished I could put myself in a similar trance, numbing my emotions. I now know that I needed to feel everything I felt – the good, the bad, the ugly, the beautiful – in order to be where I am now.

It took months of therapy for me to accept that I was not the cause and am not responsible for his actions. That no matter how much I hurt him, didn't help him, didn't hurt him, did help him (maybe helped too much?) – *whatever* – we're each solely responsible for ourselves. Obviously, our actions have consequences and do affect others, but ultimately, we are responsible for our own actions and our own happiness. It was time to own *my* happiness, to find joy within myself rather than solely through helping others find theirs.

The new, self-loving Caroline can admit that sometimes (hell, most of the time) she isn't the cool girlfriend. Instead of burying my insecurities, I've learned to hold them in my hand and examine them. If something makes me uncomfortable I either try to figure out why or I just admit that I'm not sure why I don't like it but that's okay and I am allowed to choose to avoid it. I've become better about using my yoga skills off my mat: when things come up for me, I take a few breaths, notice how I'm feeling and where it's coming from. I don't have to pretend it's not there like I used to. I don't have to pretend everything is okay so I can be there for someone else. I trust my intuition with people, environments, and situations. I trust that even if I may feel crazy at times, I'm the only person who has to live with this crazy, so I might as well accept it and love it. Journaling helps a lot. Just writing things down and getting them out of my head allows me to approach things more objectively. Rest and down-time are more important to me than ever. As an always-on-the-go helper, it can be hard for me to admit when I'm tired or need something, and scheduling naps, alone time to read or watch Netflix, or long walks in nature have been a huge saving grace for me.

It's not easy to change patterns you've spent 30 years building. I still find myself wanting to do things for others even when they're not necessarily the best things for me. I'm a lot less helpful to others but a lot more helpful to myself. That feels so much more authentic to me.

I finally feel awake.

CHAPTER 15

EMPOWERMENT

Rose Gibson

"She made no apologies for her wild heart. She left normal and regular to explore the outskirts of magical and extraordinary." ~ Michelle Rose Gilman

It was one of those glorious, Southern California autumn days boasting a cloudless blue sky, near perfect temperatures and a cool, gentle breeze blowing in from the Pacific Ocean. As my husband, fifth-grade daughter, and I walked along the sidewalk in our urban neighborhood on this mid-week day, we appeared to be a typical upper-middle class family enjoying the luxury of a late afternoon stroll. Appearances can be deceiving.

We were, in fact, a family in crisis, and our seemingly perfect life was about to implode.

Inconsistent with the normal routine, he and I went together that day to pick up our eldest of three children, age 10, from her after-school activity. Our walk back to the car transitioned from leisurely to anxiously hurried. Abruptly, he picked up my daughter and carried her on his chest as though she were a small child. The look on her face clearly indicated confusion caused by our out-of-the-ordinary actions. He angrily and harshly whispered into her ear. She started to wail. A visceral, gut-wrenching, "Noooooo!" erupted from deep within.

He was telling her something of great magnitude, of an impending action over which she would have no control, that would forever change her life. He was telling her we were getting a divorce.

"Stop it!" I yelled at him, racing to catch up as he moved faster and faster.

There had been a seeming lifetime of being ignored by him. This critical moment was no different. My feelings of being voiceless in this relationship were so ingrained in my psyche that I no longer recognized their existence. The concept that what I said actually mattered was one buried in a deep, dark place best (and safer) to never look at or give any thought to. What I said didn't matter, at least not to him. I felt so powerless that I had simply given up trying to change, trying to be heard, and this behavior where I spoke and he refused to listen had become one of many emotionally abusive patterns in our marriage.

Once at home, he assembled our children on the sofa, all lined up in a row, and proceeded to tell these young, impressionable children, ages 10, 7 and 5, outright lies.

"Your mother is having an affair!" he shouted. Three small faces crumbled into tears. "She doesn't love us anymore," his voice, fueled by anger, gained momentum. "She is leaving us for someone else!"

Amid their cries and wails, and his far-fetched, baseless accusations, my ineffective words fell on deaf ears: "Stop it! That's not true! Stop saying these things to the children!" I impotently stood there at his side. He continued ranting, repeating, going on and on, trying to assuage his hurt and damaged ego by vilifying me.

Love at First Sight

Thirty-nine years prior to that moment, Ken and I met at college. He was a senior. I was a sophomore. We started dating, and within a short time I perceived him to be the "love of my life." He earned a degree in economics and later an MBA. My degree was in art history and later my work experience would center around the non-profit contemporary art field. We dated exclusively for four years and then married. I felt no passion to pursue a career and instead focused my attention on being wife and mother, raising a family, managing a household.

Part-time work and volunteer activities enabled me to maintain some sense of identity outside of my family unit. At the time of our marriage, I was still an unformed adult. I had not truly figured out who I was at this point in my life. In fact, neither of us understood the concept of individuation (being independent, separate entities within the marriage). We had a codependent relationship that evolved into an emotionally abusive one. It was important to me to do and be something outside of my nuclear family, to feed a passion for art and culture and to foster connection within the community.

In the early days of our marriage, Ken was the love of my life. I looked up to him, admired him, wanted to be with him all of the time. I could not imagine a life without him. We waited, at my insistence, seven years after we married to begin a family.

Once, one of my girlfriends queried, "Why are you waiting so long to have children?"

The question gave me pause. "I guess," I slowly responded, "I'm not yet ready to share him." I wasn't able to articulate further, but looking back, I now see I wasn't receiving the quantity and quality of love from him that I wanted and deserved. To bring a third party (our child) into the equation was going to dilute the already-limited pool of love he had to give me.

Over the course of the next seven years, we had three children and moved into an historic five-bedroom home in an upscale neighborhood in our Southern California city. The investment firm my husband founded, around the time of our first child's birth, experienced from its inception an upward trajectory of business opportunities and financial success.

Inside the Marriage

Throughout the course of our codependent, emotionally abusive relationship, one of the things that I learned was that I was rarely going to "win" an argument with Ken. Now let me be clear, it is my opinion that a relationship is an equal partnership that entails compromise rather than "winning and losing." It's demoralizing to constantly feel like the *Loser*. And really, why, in a marriage, would one want to constantly feel like the *Winner*? So, I formed the habit of simply keeping my mouth shut rather than verbally articulating my disagreement with his point of view.

We had a close friendship with another couple, Jane and Bill. They often came over for an evening visit or dinner with the two of us. We shared a connection as neighbors, and the husbands shared a love of golf. Recently, Jane had taken up the sport to spend more time with her golf-playing husband, and, as my husband enjoyed regular golf-playing days, I became the only person in the group with no story to share and with actually no interest in the subject of golf. On one occasion, the conversation at dinner started with a particular story about a golf experience. One golf story led to another. I sat quietly, eating my dinner in silence. Feeling excluded and invisible. At the conclusion of the main course, I was so frustrated to be left out of the conversation and out of the group that I removed myself from the table. I quietly got up and left the room. There was no acknowledgment of my departure. I took a slow walk through my house, perusing all the books in the numerous bookshelves. Looked out each of the windows of the living room. Meandered up the stairs. Checked in with the sitter and my three children, who were at this point taking baths and getting ready for bed. Eventually, I made my way back downstairs and to the dinner table. The conversation was on the same story as when I had departed, likely 45 minutes prior. There was no visible notice of my return. The story continued to be told. I sat there once again in silence.

Later, I gently and cautiously approached my husband (walking on eggshells was an activity I had become adept at). "I am wondering if we might agree to put a 15-minute moratorium on the subject of golf when we meet with Jane and Bill? I feel so excluded when the three of you speak at length about golf – it's something I have no knowledge or experience of." At the conclusion of our chat, I felt as though my husband had heard me, and would be considerate of my feelings in the future.

The next time our friends came over, Bill made a grand gesture of pointing to his watch and starting a timer for fifteen minutes. *Wow*, I thought to myself, *the private conversation between Ken and me, about my feelings, had simply become fodder for a joke, of which I am now the butt, within our group of four.* I often felt invisible in the outside world. Now I felt invisible and without importance inside my home as well, in this place that was supposed to be my oasis and sanctuary. Sometimes I wondered if it would be better for all if I were simply no longer here.

The disrespect I received from my husband seeped into other relationships. Somehow, I was giving permission to everyone coming in to my home to treat me poorly. On one occasion, my husband was away on a business trip, skiing in Vail. His parents, Pam and Bob, had come for a visit while he was away. It was dinner time. The three of us were at the kitchen table, a very small, intimate space, with my father-in-law across the table from me, my mother-in-law between us.

My father-in-law looked over to his wife and said, "Pam, ask Rose if she wants the butter," pushing the butter dish toward her.

What the heck?! I thought to myself, since Silence had become my way of staying safe. *Why doesn't he just ask me myself? I'm sitting right here!*

On another occasion, my in-laws were once again visiting. This time, they planned to care for the kids while my husband and I went away. Our upcoming getaway was a huge victory on my part. Ken was regularly making business trips that occurred on the ski slopes, and participating in bachelor party weekends to places such as New Orleans and Las Vegas. I was happy for my husband to have these opportunities to travel and spend time with his friends. My wish and request were simply that on occasion he would express an interest in planning a trip with *me*. One of my primary love languages is quality time.

His regular answer to my request that we go away together was, "We have three kids!"

"Well, yes," I agreed, "but we have an au pair living at our house, and your parents are willing to come help out." For some unknown reason, he still wanted one of the actual parents to be with the kids at all times, which of course meant me.

After much pleading on my part, he relented, and we were now going to embark on a short trip. Several days before our departure, I was giving my in-laws the run down on a few things they needed to know in our absence. The three of us were standing in the hallway, within close proximity to each other, having this conversation.

Bob looked at Pam, and spoke assertively, "Tell Rose we are going to need to have a set of keys to the car!"

Enough already! I thought to myself. This time I spoke up. "Bob!" I huffed in an exasperated tone, "I'm standing right here. You can speak directly to me!"

"Ok," he responded with a sneer. He glanced down at the designer jeans I was wearing – the kind where you pay extra to have the holes and distressed markings artfully blended in to the fabric. "You need a new pair of jeans." And he abruptly turned his back on me and walked away.

So, what is it about ME, I wondered to myself, *that causes me to be treated in these dismissive and demeaning ways?* Throughout the marriage, I was constantly racking my brain to think of ways that I could make changes to improve our relationship. An unidentified, intuitive feeling told me that he was not going to truly change in a meaningful, long-term way, so instead I imagined how or what I could change in myself or in my behavior or in our patterns.

Resolving our issues through divorce, up to this point, never crossed my mind. I had agreed to marry this person, and I was going to figure out how to make this relationship better for me. That's right, I said better for "me." As far as I know, he was generally content with the relationship. He was in possession of an attractive, devoted wife, who made herself available to him, kept herself fit and healthy, lovingly tended to the children, adeptly managed a large household, cooked nutritious and wholesome meals, maintained an immaculate house, capably performed hostess duties with finesse and style, and ensured the scheduling of weekly date nights for intellectual and emotional connection. So, there I was, going down this path, living this life without much self-awareness or self-introspection. I was completely unaware of my extreme depression and increasing resentment toward my husband.

In retrospect, I can see that my efforts to present a "perfect" picture of myself to the world was my way of controlling something in a life where I felt I had little control or empowerment, or even any kind of real voice. I never left the house without a fully made-up face and impeccably-coiffed hair. I dressed in the latest fashions — completely armored head to toe with accessories and heels. Even at home I maintained this image of perfection. I could not let down my guard for a minute. There was no relaxing, letting go, letting loose. It was inconceivable to me to own a set of sweat pants or comfy clothes. So flawlessly did I present this idea of Martha Stewart-type perfection in my household, a friend later confessed to me that the first time she attended a party at my house, she sneaked into the kitchen, convinced she was going to find freshly-baked pies cooling on the window sill! While I may have projected the image of a woman who enviably (to some) seemed to have it all together, inside I felt empty and alone. Even while in the company of my husband, I felt desperately lonely.

We were upwardly mobile, seemingly unstoppable and presenting the façade of a perfect life. Ken's business dealings continued to be successful; we increased our possessions at a rapid rate and enjoyed numerous affluent activities, such as family trips to Hawaii, ski resorts, and seaside vacation rentals. My personal shopper provided me an enormous wardrobe of designer-label clothes. I worked out at my home several times a week one-on-one with a trainer to achieve the perfect body. Outwardly, we seemed to have an enviable existence, living large with a beautifully-decorated home, a nanny to assist with the care of our three children, luxurious cars, an ongoing calendar of catered parties. And yet, there was this nagging, uncomfortable yet unnamed feeling within me. With all the affluence surrounding me, why wasn't I feeling genuinely happy, fulfilled? What was wrong with my life? What was wrong with me? And then, an event occurred that served as a catalyst to forever change my life. Well, it wasn't one major event, like a lightning bolt hitting me. It was more that this *thing* happened and there was the subsequent evolution of *me* over a series of months. And years. And that evolution is one that continues to this day.

A Catalyst for Change

I met someone. A man. Yes, he was single and handsome. We were introduced at his place of business, and had opportunity to talk at length. Over the course of a year, I realized I had an attraction for him – his listening skills were a big part of the attraction. He practiced active listening, a communication technique used in counseling, training, and conflict resolution. It requires that the listener fully concentrate, understand, respond and then remember what is being said.

This may have been the first time in my life that I truly felt heard and that someone was trying to understand me. I started to believe that what I said actually mattered. Believing that I was being heard caused me to feel also that I was being seen. Not only *what* I said mattered, *who* I was mattered. And that begged the question, who was I, exactly?

What did the appearance of this person in my life mean for me? This was my first *Awakening Experience*. I began to see the world differently. At this moment in my life, what was behind me was familiar – the unknown that lay ahead felt unimaginably scary. But now the veil was lifted from my eyes, and there was no possibility of going back, living as before. I clearly heard a voice from deep within, telling me to pursue *change*, at all costs. I felt as though my life depended on the drastic change that would result from Divorce. I needed to live a life my Soul demanded, and I could not envision being that soul-driven person or living that soul-driven life in the constraints of my marriage to a materialistic, ego-driven, narcissistic, emotionally abusive husband.

At first, this anxiety-provoking idea of change made me physically ill. I quickly dropped ten pounds from lack of appetite and suffered from insomnia. But I am a determined soul and so forged on, despite all the roadblocks in my way. Those roadblocks were in the form of spouse, family, friends, finances. Those roadblocks seemed strong and powerful, hurtling toward me full force, trying to convince me that I was misguided, I was losing my sanity, I was selfish, I would fail. There was an increasingly loud voice (Hello, Higher Self) emerging from inside, guiding me along, assisting me in finding the way to what is My Truth.

My face-to-face, one-on-one interactions with this man who appeared in my life could be counted on one hand. Phone conversations with him, however, logged numerous hours. In fact, I solicited the aid of a friend to obtain a secret cell phone so that I could talk to him without my husband seeing details of our many and lengthy conversations on the phone bill that arrived monthly at his office. What did this man have to say that was so important to me? He introduced me to new, unconventional ways of thinking, to concepts that are embraced by New Age Spirituality, such as "thoughts become things" and "you create your own reality." He suggested titles of books that I proceeded to purchase and read with avid interest to absorb these brand-new (to me) concepts. We talked at length about my relationship with my husband. Those conversations enabled me for the first time to see more objectively our emotional and behavioral patterns that were in no way healthy.

Ken sensed that something was amiss. My behavior and thought patterns started to shift. I began to speak up, in small ways, to him. I exhibited obvious discomfort when this man's name came up in conversation. Ken was so troubled by the changes in me that he engaged the services of a private detective. My husband felt that I was being brainwashed and manipulated for nefarious purposes, and thus this man must be thoroughly investigated.

Where Do I Belong and Who is My Tribe?

To back up for just a minute, let me tell you that I grew up as the middle of three children. Around the age of seven, I would claim on more than one occasion that there had been a mistake when I was born, that my parents took the wrong baby home from the hospital. I felt like an outsider from a very early age. At times during my marriage when my husband and I would visit my family - parents, siblings, spouses - at my childhood home, I *still* felt like the outsider, that my husband somehow belonged with this group of people and I was the one on the outer edge. Fourteen years post-divorce, at the time of writing this chapter, I still feel that Ken owns a permanent place in my family, and my own position is the one that remains tentative.

Very recently, a personal relationship was in distress and I felt greatly saddened. This event coincided with a trip to visit my parents in my hometown. After a long day's travel, I arrived in a teary state. For the next 24 hours, my tears flowed regularly and I made no effort to hold them back. I asked for nothing from my parents, other than to be allowed to simply experience my feelings of sorrow in a place that I believed to be safe. On the second day of the visit, however, my mom sat me down to discuss my state of mind and emotions.

"Let's have a little chat. It seems like you have been looking for peace for a very long time and you can't find it," she began. "And now, you are walking around like you have a black cloud over your head." (Queue up the image of a cartoon character with a perennial cloud of rain pouring down on him. All the other characters in the comic strip are standing in the sunshine. It's this poor Loser who suffers the humiliation of rain on a sunny day.)

"Really, Mom, couldn't you simply say that you see I am very sad?" The unspoken end of her sentence seemed to say that my emotional state was making my parents feel uncomfortable in their own house and they wanted me to stop the crying. Still to this day it is neither safe nor productive to articulate my feelings.

At this moment I thought, "I am in a state of grief. If my sadness had been caused by the death of a loved one, would she then accuse me of walking around with a black cloud over my head?"

Our family's long-standing pattern is the expectation that I keep my feelings to myself, and thus, early on, I developed a protective measure of appearing perfect on the outside. This pattern manifested in my constant need to control my body (weight) and my outward appearance (clothes, hair, makeup). In fact, during marriage counseling, the therapist pointed out that whenever I expressed anger, I smiled.

For so long, I was not surrounded by like-minded, supportive people who *got me* – I was not in the right Tribe. These feelings of marginalization were like a low-grade fever. Uncomfortable, but not *yet* reaching the severe, spiking temperature that would spur me to action, compel me to make drastic life-changing decisions. The man I met served as that catalyst of change.

At the time that I met him and felt a powerful need to talk to him, very few people understood what I was going through. I don't think even *I* intuited what I was going through. I just knew that the veil had come away from my eyes. I had been metaphorically banging my head against a wall for twenty years in my marriage, asking my husband to hear me, to validate me, to love and respect me in certain and specific ways.

For example, on the occasion of our tenth wedding anniversary, I suggested to Ken, "Rather than give each other gifts, why don't we make a list of ten things we love about the other, and then exchange lists?"

His answer was unhesitant and immediate and without further explanation, "No."

At this point in time, I was on the verge of turning forty, and had no interest in futilely banging my head against a wall for another two decades.

My husband at that time said, "You are just having a mid-life crisis. Maybe some antidepressants will help. You are not happy in this home? What if we just buy a new house and move?"

At social gatherings with other couples, I started to pay acute attention to the content of our conversations. More often than not, the dominant subject matter was about material things. "You've had that BMW for three years," one of the men said to my husband. "When are you going to get a new car? Time to upgrade!"

Friends we spent time with were of my husband's choosing. The friends I chose were not living at the same economic level as we were, and thus my husband had no interest in seeing them socially.

Was I living a life that I no longer wanted? Were my activities and conversations meaningful and uplifting, or shallow and prestige-driven? Was I being the partner I wanted to be? Was I being loved the way I wanted? Were my husband and I creating an equal partnership filled with respect, listening, support? Did we even *like* each other anymore? These questions constantly filled my head and I searched desperately for answers.

I made the difficult decision to move out of the house, with the intention that by creating space between my husband and me, it would allow room for me to figure out what I was going to do – continue to work on the marriage? File for divorce? At one point prior to my departure, he and I had a prolonged and intense argument. Toward the end of our tirade, he pulled up a chair next to where I was sitting, and placed his head in my lap. This was perhaps the second time in our 21-year relationship that I had seen him cry.

As he lay there, humble and vulnerable, tears streaming down his face, he quietly whispered, "Please don't make a jackass out of me."

Suddenly, the blood flowing through my body turned to ice. He was not speaking of my value to him, how his life might be impacted if I were to leave, of the depths of the love held for me. No, what I heard was his Ego, front and center and loud and clear, expressing the embarrassment he would experience in the eyes of the rest of the world should I leave him.

We made an appointment with a children's therapist to discuss how we might best handle our situation, telling the children what was going on in the family. My husband wanted to tell the children in depth and in detail what he believed to be true, that I was having an affair and this divorce was solely because of my actions and my wishes. She advised him against this course of action. His response to her was, "I respectfully disagree." We did not return to see this therapist for advice.

During our final session with a marriage counselor, after about four months of regular sessions, we discussed a friend of mine. She would come over regularly to my apartment when I had custody of the children. He was adamantly opposed to the children's exposure to her, the reason being that, through her, I had met the man that my husband was convinced I was carrying on an affair with, and thus she was a bad influence on the children. Our marriage counselor said that he had no right to make decisions like that when the children were in my custody. There was no response from him.

"Ken," she raised her voice a small iota, "are you listening to me?"

"No," he responded resolutely. "I am tuning you out."

That moment settled everything for me. If my husband refused to listen to the advice of the professional we were paying to assist us in navigating better communication between us, I could see there was no way he would ever listen to me. I was done.

The man who showed up in my life was simply a catalyst: he opened a door for me, then exited my life almost as quickly as he had entered. When I made the difficult and painful decision to leave my marriage, I did so for a number of reasons: not being heard; not being shown love in the way I wanted; having love withheld from me as a means of punishment for perceived infractions; being treated dismissively and discourteously. I was evolving to become a person who was no longer compatible with my husband or the life we were creating together. I was headed down an unknown path that was vastly different from the one I had been traveling on for my entire life up to this point (which now felt like a Stepford Wives-type of existence), and my desire to change was not in sync with what others thought I should be doing.

I preferred to be alone (meaning not in this marriage) unencumbered by the limiting, choking relationship I had with my husband, looking for the kind of love that I wanted and knew I deserved, rather than feel trapped in a situation that I believed would never improve.

Alone. Alone. Alone. That's certainly how I felt. My parents, one sibling, and friends sided with my ex-husband for a number of years, ostracizing me for my decision to divorce.

Crime and Punishment

The desire to change my life, or walk a new and different path, was met with resistance on all sides. My family, for the most part, sided with my ex-husband. Friends fell away. On more than one occasion I was pointedly ignored when passing by a "friend" on the street. One time, I arrived at the door of the house that I had moved out of, to pick up our youngest child for the day. It was early in the morning and the other two were getting ready to go to school. I wanted to come in to the house to say hello to them. My youngest child had come out of the house and was standing near me. Anticipating opposition from my husband, I placed my foot in the door jamb and made my request to come in to say hello. He refused. I did not move. He attempted to shut the door, slamming it repeatedly against my foot, and, seeing how this was proving ineffective, started to kick my foot and leg. At that moment, my oldest child came up behind him and saw what he was doing. My youngest one, next to me, also stood there wide-eyed in disbelief. The oldest one made a loud gasp and ran further into the house and up the stairs.

"See what you made the kids witness!" he shouted angrily at me before slamming the door in my face.

As I drove away, I could see my oldest child standing at the window of her second-floor bedroom, silently and gravely waving to me. After this incident, he forbade me to step foot on the property and I was forced to ring the bell on the outside gate to announce my arrival to pick up the children.

How Did This Awakening Change My Life?

It takes great inner strength to forge ahead when you are ostracized by the people you thought were members of your tribe.

I was once asked, "If you had known ahead of time how difficult this process of divorce and starting a new life was going to be, wouldn't you have chosen to stay?"

The answer comes quickly and emphatically, "Absolutely not!"

What did I have before my Awakening? Previously, I was maintaining the status quo, mechanically going through the motions of life. I felt like I was constantly walking on eggshells, and carefully thought out my words before I spoke to my husband. There was a pervasive but unrecognized fear of his reaction to what I might want to say. It was a flat-line existence, and one where I never challenged myself. I stayed, trapped and hopeless, within the box that I had created for myself.

What do I have now? My life may not be perfect, but it is authentic and a life of my own choosing. I now have unencumbered freedom to explore and to discover who I am. The awakening process gives me the impetus to act, to move forward in spite of my fear. The fear is still there, but it is no longer stopping me from truly living and thriving, as opposed to merely existing. That exploration has taken me to places such as Haiti and Morocco, to attend Soul Retreats and Shaman-led earth healing classes, to experiment with dancing and drumming to move the energy and emotions within my body.

Spirituality – connection to Source – is now a primary focus in my daily life. I live the principles of feng shui that I teach and practice: connecting with nature, breathing, focusing on experiences rather than material things. Simplicity. Speaking up for myself. Surrounding myself with my *tribe* – like-minded individuals who believe in the Abundance of the Universe, a concept that takes us to a place of generosity rather than competition.

The awakening process is an ongoing one. For me, twelve years after my marriage ended, I crossed another threshold that exponentially opened my heart, mind and soul to further expanded consciousness. My life path took me to Ireland where I studied feng shui, and subsequently started an environmental energy healing business. My exposure to and study of energy healing has felt like someone pressed the Fast Forward button on my spiritual growth program. I see more clearly now.

For example, two of my children are not speaking to me or coming around to see me. One child perhaps feels that I have evolved into such a vastly different person, with all the feng shui fountains I have placed in the house, and positive affirmations posted in various locations, and my talk of energy healing, that he just doesn't get me and cannot see the importance of spending time with me. The other one, I wonder if she is angry about something that goes very deep, since she has decided for the moment to cut me out of her life. After initially taking her behavior personally, and for several weeks of crying over the loss of my child and our relationship, I woke up to the realization that her behavior mirrors that of my former husband. She made a decision based on her own alternative reality that I had done something wrong and her punishment was to withhold her love from me. I suffered that type of emotional abuse from my ex-husband for twenty years. My *awakening process*, and the subsequent personal work I have done, have given me the tools and the strength to see that the anger projected onto me has nothing to do with me! **Love and happiness come from within, not from external places or people.**

The difference for me now is that I am no longer taking things so personally. I see that my kids are in pain. Their response to the pain is misguided. Separating one's self entirely from a loved one as a means of punishment equals emotional abuse. I can now see patterns of behavior where I could not see them before. The internal growth I have worked so hard to achieve allows me to continue to be loving toward my children, yet stand firm with my boundaries, and to refuse to accept any kind of abuse, no matter who it is coming from.

Some awakening experiences might cause someone to *remember* who they *are*. I am in the process of simply *discovering* who I *am*. I am not invisible. What I say and do indeed matter. Greatly. I am a Divine Light Being, as we all are, and it is important to shine my light in this world. How I do that, well, I am still discovering what that looks like, on a daily basis. It is an ongoing process and one that is meant to be enjoyed, and relished, moment to moment. Because that is what this is all about, our time here on this planet – the adventure, the journey, the discovery, the experiences, the human connection.

I hope to evoke in others the courage to make the necessary changes they need to make in their lives despite the fear or the discomfort or the challenges. We all have a fire within our soul. We can choose to turn the flame down and live within self-imposed boundaries in order to stay safe and quiet. Or we can fan that flame and take leaps into the unknown, to explore our inner self and outer world, to embrace evolution, to embrace the Wild Heart.

CHAPTER 16

AWARENESS

Katy Hughes

I peered down the endless, dimly lit high school hallway. I could barely make out the shadows in the distance but heard the muffled sounds of people talking. I looked up at her and said, "Mom...when is Dad coming out?"

"When they are done in the locker room," she replied.

Everyone knows that kids have no sense of time, so at age four that could be tomorrow for all I knew. This was our standard family drill which dates back as far as I can remember: me waiting to spend time with my Dad and learning at an early age that his priorities were different from mine. My father has a passion for football, a game that is the center of his universe which appears to make him completely unavailable for six months of the year – or maybe that's just my emotional response to him.

While I was growing up, my Dad was a solid provider. He was a counselor, the dean, and a football coach, then worked construction during summer breaks to make ends meet since both my parents were high school counselors with modest salaries. That said, there was no substitute for "time spent" which I've learned is my love language, and a gap that would continue to haunt me in every adult relationship I created well into my 40s. To him, he was doing what he loved as he played football in college and went on to be a career coach after graduation. To me, he was an absent, unavailable father who could only connect through sports. Looking back, I can see clear as day the patterns that began sometime in middle school.

I was a busy child who loved to laugh and was full of energy. I looked for any chance to play outside that blew off steam and run around with the neighborhood kids which I believe led to a collegiate track career. It was my running around that made me feel alive and free, whether I was running down the block chasing someone playing flashlight tag, or riding my bike pedaling as fast as I could to be the first one down the hill back to our driveway. Ready, set, go! I was always up for the challenge with anyone who wanted to take me on. I became that kid who was always ready to play no matter what the game or who was playing. Determined to win at all costs, I felt most alive when I could hear my heart pounding in my ears and feel it beating fast in my chest as the beads of sweat would stream down my back. That was living in my book and the early start of my life-long adrenaline fix.

As I got older, I learned that the tone at our house was dictated by my Dad's mood driven by whether his football team won or lost their weekend game. This scale ranged from ecstatic, giddy, and euphoric when they won to life-ending screaming and his being unapproachable after a loss: "What do you mean your homework isn't done? Why do I have to tell you one hundred times to do something? Do I need to get my belt?" It was quite an emotional rollercoaster to manage as I worked hard to keep my behavior in check and avoid any type of blowout. I would liken his behavior to someone who is addicted to drugs and needs a regular fix or, in this case, his next win.

It's no wonder I spent most of my life living in extremes while I ran my body into the ground through sports to feel better about myself. Instead of learning about self-care and how to love myself for the amazing person I was, I often judged my self-worth and everything in my life by fitness levels, winning, and losing - just as he did. The silver lining is I did pick up his strong work ethic, so I have been a successful team player in various sports and later used that trait to create a successful career. Unfortunately, that did not translate well into my personal life, the place where I would learn my most difficult life lessons.

Thus, I've spent most of my life using sports as a tool to manage stress, to find peace, and to hide from life. From playing three sports in high school to running track in college, and now a sprint triathlete for the last 20+ years, the fitness benefits have been positive when they are balanced. When left unchecked, however, the body takes the brunt of that beating and eventually shuts down offering a sharp reminder of emotional pain. Add a masculine type A+ personality into the mix, and that get-it-done mentality ended up driving unrealistic expectations around goals and successful outcomes.

While drive is also a great trait, since a strong work ethic is required to reach any level of achievement, it is this type of driven mindset that opened the door for crash-and-burn behavior patterns from my subconscious. I've worked hard, I've struggled, and I've been fortunate to reap the rewards of all that hard work, but it didn't come without a price. With a successful career, financial security, a collection of triathlon medals, trophies, plaques, and two divorces under my belt, at age 40 I started to become painfully aware of the damage I had done to my body over time and the cumulative cost for my lack of personal tools and coping skills.

Three years after my college graduation, I married my high school sweetheart after several attempts at a long-distance relationship. We moved across country to start our new life together and after several career changes, relocations, and advanced degrees, our marriage ended in my late 20s when I divorced him after years of emotional disconnection. Then in my mid-30s, I married my second husband and we decided to start our own family. Having been a stepmom to his young son for several years, I welcomed the challenge to have my own child.

At age 39, we decided to visit an IVF clinic running the usual battery of tests to identify the root cause of our delay. Then on the morning of my 40th birthday, I found myself sitting alone shivering in a paper-thin gown on the exam table as my mind raced while waiting for the test results. When the doctor re-appeared, he had a concerned look on his face and what came out of his mouth was something no one is prepared for.

"You've tested positive for ovarian cancer," he said quietly in a sad tone. I could feel the knots forming in my stomach and my heart began to pound as if I would go into cardiac arrest right there on the table.

Then, after the moment of shock subsided, I snapped, "I'm sorry, what did you just say?" with squinted eyes. This death sentence was not my idea of the best way to celebrate my milestone birthday. I became impatient, leaned toward him in attack mode, and started to challenge his announcement with a barrage of questions.

"How is this possible with no symptoms? Which test points to that diagnosis? How often is this test a false positive? I don't have cancer!" I barked in rambling disbelief. How could a person have cancer and not have one single symptom? I couldn't wrap my head around it logically, so I just dismissed it. I didn't want to shoot the messenger, so I quickly got myself under control, dressed, and started to walk towards the door.

He began again, "Your numbers are abnormally high for the C125 blood test which is an indicator of cancer. Your best option is an OB GYN oncology practice referral for additional testing." I was two steps away from losing all rational thought when I took a deep breath, cut him off, and said, "Thanks for your time," and walked out.

What was more telling was that my husband was unfazed by the news at home later that evening. Ironically, he didn't hesitate to tell me on more than one occasion that his swimmers were healthy, and that I was the reason our plan was failing.

"How did your tests go today?" he yelled from the couch as he watched television in the kitchen. I could feel my irritation quickly heat up and start to boil in my stomach like a hot tea kettle. The muscle knots immediately began to form as the fire in my belly now was raging like a late-night campground blaze. I was extremely hurt that he didn't make time to attend this critical medical appointment - especially on my birthday.

"I have ovarian cancer, how's that for birthday news?" I sarcastically replied.

He looked at me with a cold hollow robotic stare and said, "So what are you going to do now?" then turned his head back toward the TV. He clearly couldn't be bothered as that was painfully obvious from his emotionless reaction to his wife's life-threatening disease. The conversation felt like something experienced at the grocery store sharing pleasantries during checkout discussing the challenge of preparing for bad weather with the clerk before walking away with no attachment.

It was at that point the wheels on the tour bus of my life started to come off one at a time, careening in DUI-like fashion. A confirmed diagnosis soon followed from the oncology specialist and I learned that endometriosis has the same characteristics as ovarian cancer. Over the next seven years a series of surgeries would be needed to address this hideous disease that affects more than 5 million women today. Immediately following the first of three outpatient procedures, my second marriage ended as my husband finally owned up to the affair he was having at work the past several months. Regardless of the doctor's assurance of a full recovery, I no longer had any interest to procreate with this man and was thankful that God had intervened on my behalf. I was not surprised to learn my intuition about his affair was spot on, however, I had yet again attracted another man into my life who was emotionally unavailable and not committed to our relationship.

During the shellshock of that year, I decided it was time to rebuild once again and focus on learning why I continued to attract men who were unavailable with commitment issues. I was determined not to repeat the Jerry Springer episode I lived: I got into counseling, read books, wrote journals, penned letters to my father that I never sent, reconnected with my inner child all in a desperate attempt to change my life. I was determined to correct this gap that continued to surface as I wanted some normalcy and to find a partner I could connect with emotionally who would support my needs.

To help create change, I accepted an amazing career opportunity that included global travel. For the next two years, I visited close to 20 countries, met some amazing people, experienced several cultures, and learned more during that job stint than many do in a lifetime. While traveling to many Eastern countries, I began to learn more about alternative healing methods while I read books about conscious awareness and spiritual journeys. I finally started to unravel the bigger issue – I was the problem. Over time, I had slowly shut down emotionally and had become disconnected from myself, my feelings, my needs and thus, I was attracting the same into my life. The next three years as I read and dated, I thought I was moving toward reconnecting to myself emotionally only to learn that I continued to repeat the pattern.

While exciting, the global circuit soon became exhausting. Since I was never home, it created more disconnection on many levels. Plus, I was healthy again and knee deep in triathlon training all over the globe in hotel gyms, high rise pools, and running on the streets of the countries I visited. It's amazing how the mind will settle back into old familiar patterns in the blink of an eye, and, this time, it was during a three-week trip to Asia that another medical crash surfaced as my body tried to raise the white flag and surrender again.

The night before I flew to New Delhi, I found myself on my bathroom floor of the Westin Hotel in Thailand at 2 a.m. after finishing a week of charity work with friends. I was the last of the group to leave since I was going on to India for business. I was sick and alone and thousands of miles away from the comfort of friends or family.

As I stared at the toilet water between heaves with tears running down my face and a cold rag on my neck, I sobbed, "God, please help me live through this nightmare. I don't want to die in Thailand." I curled up in the fetal position sweaty and feverish on the floor for the next several hours near the toilet so the energy to manage this repeated cycle required minimal effort to lift my head. After the realization that I was hit with food poisoning, I now had a bigger crisis on my hands to manage: how am I going to fly to India all day tomorrow and not get sick on the plane? Will there be enough sick sacks? Will someone help me? It's amazing what I have been able to live through when there is no other choice. I eventually made it through the trip, but the aftershock seemed to linger as my stomach took months to heal no matter what I did. I thought I was conscious and had learned how to handle my emotional stress. Instead, I subconsciously ignored this second wake-up call.

Then, one day on a business trip to Dubai, I woke up and wasn't sure what time zone I was on or which country I was in. I decided it was time to get off the global circuit. Soon after that epiphany, like clockwork, a LinkedIn recruiter called me with a new role at Microsoft - the holy grail of jobs. Off I went to start my new chapter which seemed like the perfect opportunity to start over again. *Ready, set, go!* I thought. Go, go, go, work, work, work, train, train, train, before the next crash.

Three months into my new job, rinse-repeat resurfaced, but this time I had met a man with whom I had a connection like no other. I thought, *This time it's different.* We talked about everything for hours, we connected on multiple levels, and I believed I'd finally reached a place of emotional awareness that allowed me to connect with someone. After two years of long-distance fairytale dating, as I call it, our relationship ended badly, and I added it to my list of emotionally unavailable casualties. If that wasn't enough, my endometriosis also had resurfaced and was extremely overwhelming, creating a slow downward spiral that included extensive amounts of alcohol to cope. A second surgery was inevitable. This time it would be a full hysterectomy which really took a toll on my body and my mental state. It also forced me to start to look at how I could begin to chip away at reconnecting with myself, instead of living in the crash-and-burn pattern I had become accustomed to.

As I sat on my couch staring down at its brown wide whale corduroy pattern, it slowly became blurry as the tears rolled down my face. It had been six years since my divorce and now feeling alone and reeling from another dysfunctional relationship, I searched my mind for answers. *What did I do to deserve all this pain? How did I get so sick?* I pleaded with myself as I sat in a state of numbness and sobbed. I never expected my life to unfold this way: divorced twice, no ability to have children, multiple surgeries to address an extensive medical issue, all before age 50.

It was like I woke up one day, looked in the mirror and said, "Who are you and what have you done with my happy?" At that moment I could feel my soul screaming at me, "HELLOOOOOOOO, are you in there?" Yes, I was in there and stuck as if trapped in cement, living my life in a rinse-repeat mode for the last 30+ years. I was asleep on autopilot listening to the same subconscious bad tape replaying itself over and over screaming, "You don't deserve to be happy!"

Some call this voice the roommate in your head, or the ego. Others aren't sure what to make of it. One thing is certain: many who are emotionally aware know that this voice should be ignored at all costs because it just generates negative self-talk. I often feel powerless when I listen to that voice or support behavior that doesn't serve me. That kind of energy doesn't come from a place of self-love. Instead it feeds on fear, uncertainty, and doubt. It was time to make a new choice: go inside and listen to my Inner Voice, not the crazy roommate in my head who thinks it has all the answers. I was finally awake, conscious, and in control of my own life.

As I continue to slowly detach from my old belief system and what I had been taught growing up, I have become the observer of my past and the things that unfold daily in my life. I now work with intuitive healers on a regular basis to release the trapped emotions I have apparently been carrying around for years in my tissues, and work hard to manage the stress that I create in my life. I still search, question, read, and talk to various like-minded friends. I try to connect regularly with my Inner Voice to find alignment with who I am, where I want to be, what I want from life, and who I want to spend my time with. I no longer want to be disconnected from my emotional well-being and work hard to make sure that doesn't happen. I felt angry and sad for years living behind a thick layer of fear-based veneer visible through the people I dated, who I worked with, my thoughts. All of it wasn't authentic and it didn't feel real, yet I kept subconsciously creating this warped reality continually.

I have come to realize that the connection I have been seeking outside was the connection to myself inside. That was the connection that has been missing all these years. It was **ME** that I wasn't connected to, my Inner Voice or Spirit, my soul, my authenticity. I had been living in a space where I was doing what I was told, following the rules, making others happy, all at my personal expense. I was coasting through life as if I was on a tour bus guided by someone else, yet I wasn't quite sure how to get off that bus. No voice, no truth, no life – no happy.

I'm not suggesting everyone should look for a life crisis, create an illness, or expect to have some sort of awakening moment to find her soul. I've just learned over the years that instead of focusing on the past and looking outside to others for fulfillment, connection, stability and love - to look within and focus on happiness that can be generated by living life in the present that you create and own. As I peel my own healing onion layer by layer, I've come to understand more about my boundaries, my needs, and why my relationship patterns were repeating. The baggage I was carrying and the belief system from my upbringing was killing my soul. Although my parents love me and did the best they could with what they had, it was time to begin a new healing journey focused on connection, forgiveness, and love, and to stop subconsciously blaming others for my unhappiness.

I started to really look at my health situation with a critical eye. Over the years, my body had taken the brunt of all my stuffed emotions and busy-stress, and it was now fighting back in full-assault mode. I had no choice but to listen or I would eventually end up in the hospital or worse, I would exit this life. The Universe continues to put new relationships in my path to test the lessons I've learned around self-love, self-care, and truly being worthy of the best that love and life offer. Now things are different as I can finally see and hear, helping me to create a healthy balance of better decisions around what I need to drive my overall happiness, and not repeat my former crash-and-burn pattern.

Once I stopped looking outside, it became very clear that I have a lot of work still to do inside. I now set aside regular time to quietly connect with myself and just listen. Call it meditation, call it a break. Regardless of the label, I have found this necessary to keep grounded during today's technology-driven rat race we call life. Instead of ignoring my gut instincts when things don't feel right, I stop, take a breath, and see what I can hear or feel. It is in this stillness that I have been able to find the peace and the answers I have been looking for guiding my life, my journey, and my purpose.

I'm not saying I have it all figured out as nothing could be further from the truth, but after years of pain, suffering, searching, and feeling alone, I have surrendered to an optimistic outlook and I am thankful for my experiences while trying to avoid subconscious outlets. I now come from a rose-colored lens of gratitude and happiness, which allows me to experience the joy in life regardless of the lessons. I'm excited to see what the future holds!

CHAPTER 17

SURRENDER

Lauren Lenore

February in Portland is almost always wet and dreary. A sunny day is a real treat, refreshing and enlivening in its simplicity. It was on one of those crisp, clear mornings, while my grandpa lay dying, that I took a moment to myself to sneak outside. The old farmhouse yard had become overgrown and messy with the years, a model of how strong and resilient nature is when left alone. It was the type of place with many secrets and a deep connection to the universe. I sat on a rock with my face turned toward the bright sun thinking about the past year and how I resembled the garden. I had been thrown into the role of caregiver not once but twice over the past twelve months. In each situation, circumstances weren't ideal, but I was the one who was there. I didn't always do the right thing, but I learned from my mistakes and grew deeper roots of who I am and what I have to offer.

The previous March I was on track to finish my MBA in a few months and had just started what I thought was a dream internship that was going to lead to a dream career with a dream company. Then, sitting on a different rock in a different city while sad drizzling rain hit my slumped shoulders, I listened as my sister told me the doctor found cancer in the tumor in my dad's neck. That's when everything started to change.

Cancer is such a ubiquitous word in our culture today. It seems the disease has affected everyone. But *my* dad? The ex-river rafting guide and relentless adventurer? The strong man constantly pushing his limits? The man who taught me to love nature and to grow my own tomatoes? How could he have cancer? I sat on the grey rock under a grey sky and let the rain mix with my tears not caring that other students were staring or blatantly looking the other way.

"I'm coming home," I told my sister. "I'll be there in three hours." It wasn't a question or a decision. I just knew I had to do it.

"But there's nothing you can do now, there's nothing any of us can do right now." She responded, not wanting me to miss class or work. She sounded tired and a little pushy as so many big sisters do when they're trying to take care of you, but there was also a little ache in her voice. Even if I couldn't help the situation, I could give her a hug and show her how grateful I was she'd been there to take the news and be strong for my dad as he learned he had cancer.

"I don't care. I need to be with him and with you and the other stuff can go to hell." Many more times over the next year, I would continue to make decisions based on what felt right in the moment and being present for what is important in life.

"He just won't listen to me," I complained to the caregiver support counselor. It was the middle of May and my dad was four weeks into his six weeks of chemo and radiation treatment. "I'm at a loss. I try so hard to help and all we end up doing is arguing. I know I'm just making it harder on him, but I feel such a need to get my point across. I feel like he discounts any of my suggestions and thinks I don't empathize with how hard it is for him. I'm not trying to put more pressure on him, but he needs to stop working and start focusing on his health and getting better but he doesn't understand where I'm coming from. I'm just so worried about him and that the negativity and stress in his life are going to kill him." My voice cracked and I could feel the tears that were always threatening from deep inside me finally explode. The counselor handed me a tissue and looked at me with compassion.

"Wow, that must be really hard on you," she said, "to be taking on so much of this burden alone."

It wasn't just the struggle with my dad's health that had me so distraught. Over the past few months, I felt like the universe just wouldn't let up. To start, a week after we found out about my dad's diagnosis, my internship was phased out and there was no longer a position for me at my "dream" company. Then I had to break someone's wonderful heart because I knew I couldn't give him what he needed and the disappointment in myself was palpable. I was becoming distanced by friends and could feel long-term friendships disintegrating but there was nothing I could do, or at least nothing I really cared to do except feel ditched by people I thought were my support network. I was falling behind in grad school and although I knew I was on track to graduate in a month, I wasn't showing up to the last term as the best version of myself and I knew it. To top it off, I had just had another relationship opportunity blow up because I had put too much pressure on it, forcing it because I saw it as the only good thing in my life. Looking back, I could see I'd convinced myself that this relationship could solve all the other issues in my life. Overall, I had been feeling like a complete failure.

"Have you thought about giving yourself a break?" the counselor asked. "Being the primary caretaker for a patient going through this kind of treatment is hard on anyone, let alone when it's for your father who you thought was invincible. You are both dealing with how your roles are shifting and it's not easy. It's a difficult situation and you both need more compassion and love for each other's positions." We were sitting in her small office of the large sterile hospital while my dad received chemotherapy upstairs. Hearing someone acknowledge out loud that it *was* hard and that it sucked but that I was doing a good job sent tears of relief flooding down my cheeks. To know that it's ok to not be ok was liberation.

That conversation opened the door for me to see my situation from a different angle. I knew I couldn't continue as I was. I was killing myself with pressure and expectations. I knew I needed to do something differently, but I didn't know how. I was *doing* everything. Something clicked while reading Pema Chodron's book *When Things Fall Apart*. Maybe that was the problem; maybe *doing* wasn't what I needed to be doing. This little thought rocked my world and started to change my perception of reality.

"I really appreciate you being here," my dad said for the third time that August morning. We were at another doctor's appointment and I was again by his side with my notebook and my binders. But this was different. This appointment was the first check-up since treatment ended in May. Today we would find out how he was healing and if all the cancer was gone.

"I know Dad. I love you and you know I wouldn't have been anywhere else these past six months," I answered honestly.

My problems hadn't miraculously disappeared since my revelation three months earlier, but I had started to give myself a break and to give my dad a break. I felt the universe responding to my efforts. I joined a meditation course at the local Buddhist center and was exploring how to control and calm my mind. In addition to Pema Chodron's book, I had been reading more about spirituality and my connection to the universe and often I had intense feelings that what I was reading was reminding me of something I already knew but hadn't remembered until reading it. It just made sense and I began to form a spiritual belief system not based on any religion or specific teaching but on what felt right to me.

Things didn't magically click into place. I'd still had some major setbacks: after eight months working together, my professional idol and mentor unexpectedly and without explanation canceled my project and completely shunned me. I was again devastated and angry at the universe. A few weeks earlier, I'd randomly clicked on a YouTube video that one of my yoga friends had published of an interview with her Reiki master. I instantly felt connected to Sharna even though I had never met her. I joined her email list-serve. Sharna was hosting a Reiki Level 1 training in San Diego in a few weeks and something told me this was my time. I easily rearranged everything and signed up to explore my connection to energy.

Diving deeper into energy work helped me realize I needed to take time to focus on trusting the universe and on my own self-healing. I started to see my life in three major buckets:

- Career/ Success
- Love/Relationships (including romantic, friends and family)
- My spirituality/Connection to the universe/Knowing my Self

I had felt so out of control because the universe was trying to show me that really there is no control. No matter the situation of our lives, we can be happy and free from worry. By focusing on filling the third bucket I was starting to understand this.

Now my dad and I were sitting in the same hospital where we'd spent so much time in the past year waiting to hear if it had all worked.

"Everything on the scans look good," the doctor said, very matter of fact.

"What?" my dad asked with such a deep level of concern and emotion in his voice I was worried. "What does that mean?"

"It means you no longer have cancer," the doctor responded, and my dad started crying.

"Dad! It's ok, you're ok." I got up to hug him and started to tell him something like, *I told you, you just needed to be positive* but there was an expression on his face I'd never seen, or at least I'd never noticed. I really hadn't realized until this moment how scared he'd been that things wouldn't turn out ok. So instead I just held his hand and we listened to the rest of the doctor's report.

As my dad's health continued to improve I went back to full-time job searching but my confidence was repeatedly broken when I was rejected by numerous job opportunities, many after two or three rounds of interviews. My commitment to the third bucket started to fall behind and again I got caught up in the anxiety of "what am I going to do with my life?"

I had fallen so far behind in my spiritual growth that I was suffering bouts of anxiety and depression that were similar to when I first felt them in high school fifteen years earlier. I no longer had my role as my dad's caretaker, that although extremely hard, had given my life purpose. I was unhappy with my current life situation but couldn't fix it. Again, I thought I was doing everything right, but I just felt stuck. I was meditating every day and eating healthy, nourishing foods. I was working on myself and my connection to the universe. I was trying so hard to trust that it would all work out the way it was supposed to, but I was impatient and angry. Why was the universe taking me so far down these paths only to lead me to a dead end? What was the lesson I was supposed to learn? What was I supposed to do with my life and why wasn't that thing clear?

It was now the end of October. My grandpa, whom I call Benny, and I were standing at the front door of his and my grandma's old farmhouse waiting for my mom to help my grandma finish getting ready for her birthday brunch. We were looking out at the grey Fall rain when he abruptly said, "I have something important I need to talk to you about, you and your mom and Matt (my uncle). I know you've noticed but there is something going on with my health and it just isn't right, I'm having some more tests but I just..." he trailed off choked by emotion. This sudden outburst shocked me. My grandpa wasn't one to show emotion and although we had grown close a few years earlier when I helped him care for my grandma after she suffered two strokes five days apart, I didn't understand why he was confiding in me first.

"Oh, Benny, it's ok." I reached out and placed my hand on his arm. "What's going on?"

"Ohf, I'll just tell you when we're all together!" He gruffly shot back, angered at his flood of emotion and lack of control of it.

A month and a half later, he was in the emergency room with severe abdominal pain and had driven himself there the night before. I was angry no one had told me. He shouldn't have to be there alone! I called the hospital and found out where he was and went to see him not caring that he wouldn't want me there. Whenever my grandma had been in the hospital over the past few years, he'd always said there's nothing anyone can do, and he was definitely not the type to want to be fussed over. But I'd learned something being in so many hospitals and at so many doctor appointments with my dad: sometimes it's just nice to know people care about you. So, I went, and I sat with him and when he asked why I was there I told him because I wanted to be and we left it at that.

After four days, two surgeries, and multiple rounds of tests and scans, my grandpa was diagnosed with an inoperable tumor. He was sent home on palliative and hospice care with less than six months to live.

My story took many more twists and turns as it became entwined with my grandpa's struggles as he faced death during the next three months. I helped him navigate the decision to control his own death through Death with Dignity, tried to comfort and buffer family challenges, handled much of the physical care help that he needed like changing the drain tube dressings and monitoring meds. It was very similar to the role I had played for my father, but I was very different. I don't know if it was the fact that my grandpa wasn't going to get better or that I had learned from the time spent as the caregiver for my dad but this time around I remembered the importance of me. With the help of reiki, meditation, and spiritual readings and classes, I processed what I was going through. I stayed present in the moments that I had with my grandpa and I started to internalize the idea that everything in our lives happens at exactly the right time, exactly as we need them to happen. I learned the importance of holding space and not trying to fix everything that is wrong but rather to see it for what it is and accept it.

Sitting outside on that morning of February 10, I was filled with gratitude. My grandfather was an amazing man. He was adventurous and stubborn and a great teacher. I was unbelievably grateful for all he had taught me, and I know it sounds cliché, but I knew he would continue to teach me and guide me whenever I need him.

The feeling of the sun on my face felt like it was pouring life back into me, filling my heart with peace. A bright flash like someone had used a mirror to magnify the sun's rays brought me back to the present moment. I opened my eyes, looked around, and shrugged. The winter chill was starting to sneak past my coat and I went back inside to my mom and grandma just getting up from the kitchen table. "Will you help Grandma to the couch while I clean up?" my mom asked, then went into the other room to look for stray dishes.

"Lauren?!??!" I hear my mom's anxious tone a few seconds later. "I think you need to get in here."

I rushed through the swinging door from the kitchen to the dining room where my grandpa had been in a coma for the past three days. Even though she hadn't said anything, I knew his spirit had finally left his body.

"Joan," I turned at my grandma's sorrow-filled voice and moved over as she slowly came up behind us.

"I think he's gone," my mom almost whispered. I leaned down and even though I already knew, I checked for a pulse and a breath. Not wanting to say it and not wanting to be wrong, I waited longer than probably necessary to confirm. "Yeah, he's gone," I said and we all started crying and holding each other as the sadness and relief and confusion and grief all intertwined through our minds and our souls. This was what he wanted, my mom and I had to remind my grandma and ourselves. He wanted to have control to not suffer and die sick and miserable. He had a good life but now he finally had his release and it was time for us to also take our next steps or at least start to figure out what those next steps would be.

Frank Sinatra's *My Way* had become Benny's theme song and as we listened to it one last time we each said goodbye.

And now, the end is near
And so I face the final curtain
My friend, I'll say it clear
I'll state my case, of which I'm certain
I've lived a life that's full

I've traveled each and every highway

But more, much more than this

I did it my way

Regrets, I've had a few

But then again, too few to mention

I did what I had to do

And saw it through without exemption

I planned each charted course

Each careful step along the byway

And more, much more than this

I did it my way

Yes, there were times, I'm sure you knew

When I bit off more than I could chew

But through it all, when there was doubt

I ate it up and spit it out

I faced it all and I stood tall

And did it my way

I've loved, I've laughed and cried

I've had my fill, my share of losing

And now, as tears subside

I find it all so amusing

To think I did all that

And may I say - not in a shy way

Oh no, oh no, not me

I did it my way

For what is a man, what has he got

If not himself, then he has naught

To say the things he truly feels

And not the words of one who kneels

The record shows I took the blows

And did it my way

Yes, it was my way

As I write this, it's been exactly two months since my grandpa's passing. And, where am I? Of course, I'm back in my life and have the three buckets vying for attention again. But my approach to them is very different than it was six months ago and unrecognizable from how it was two or three years ago. I'm trying to hold on to my connection to the universe and source energy, trusting my guides to help me along the best path that is right and true for me. I have a new job I am excited about and just connected with an interesting man that may or may not develop romantically and either way I'm ok with it. While these aspects of my life are important, I know that if they don't work out, I will be ok. I truly believe that if something doesn't work out then it wasn't meant for me. When things don't go the way I hope, it means something even better is coming. And no matter what I need to do, I'll do it my way.

CHAPTER 18

RENEWAL

Jennifer Nevarez

In my case, Awakening was more of an abrupt halt and unexpected change of course. All necessary and all good in the long haul, but in the moment, it was all a bit of a shock.

Early in the morning on August 29, 2005, Hurricane Katrina arrived in my home city of New Orleans.

The week before, I was off to San Antonio for a few days of consulting. While packing the one small carry-on I took with me, I was unaware that I was packing for life. Originally, I was scheduled to fly home Saturday, but that proved impossible as the airport closed to inbound traffic in order to accommodate the flood of refugees evacuating the city. I could not fly home to gather valuables and evacuate my belongings before the storm made landfall Monday morning, so I raced to a friend's house in Austin to wait, watch, and wonder, hunkering down for what was next.

We watched the news with nervous apprehension. The storm rolled into lower Louisiana that Monday morning. Although it was fierce and caused a great deal of damage, my neighborhood seemed to weather the storm pretty well, at first. Then, the levees broke. Torrents of flood water poured through the streets. We caught snippets of the media coverage on TV as the waters rose. Overnight, everything familiar was gone. It was clear I would not be going home.

In an instant, the simple yet massive natural force of water and wind had dissolved life as I knew it, scattering the people and places familiar to me. I was awash in shock and disbelief.

That stunned and frozen feeling that comes from disaster doesn't dissipate easily, either. It took weeks before we were allowed back into our neighborhood, which felt more like a war zone by then. Streets were barely passable and littered with mangled cars and uprooted trees. Debris was everywhere, too, and hardly a roof was intact. Due to the lack of utilities and lack of basic civil services, combined with the unfortunate danger of looting that had spread in the aftermath, there was a military curfew. We were only allowed into the city during the daylight hours to begin the long and painstakingly slow yet unhealthy work of clearing the saturated and moldy remnants of a home and a life.

After months of recovery work and scaling mountains of debris, I was upside down, grieving the decimation of all I had known while wading through the letting-go process and wondering what was next amidst the overwhelming feeling of uprootedness and lingering waves of shock.

While awash in chaos and confusion, however, old friends came out of the woodwork. Long-lost college buddies reached out to offer temporary housing, as the invisible threads of relation rose like lifelines, the web of humanity showing itself in the face of epic disaster and personal life upheaval. Thanks to the influence of a children's book author and illustrator from California, who had become a dear and treasured friend while collaborating to promote his book *Crazy Hair Day*, I got an unexpected invitation from his sister to come to New Mexico for a few days of consulting. In the face of all that debris, devastation, and disaster, I said, Yes.

Sometimes, we say Yes mysteriously, opening a door unknowingly to the most amazing change of course. That Yes takes us on a trajectory we would never have imaged or planned. In my case, I landed at the SunPort in Albuquerque and drove north an hour on Highway 25 to Santa Fe. While driving and reveling in the majesty of the rugged desert mountains, wide-open sky, and clean, fresh air of northern New Mexico, an epiphany hit me somewhere between Cochiti and La Bajada hill. I had to pull over. Call it an epiphany or even a vision, whatever happened to me was particular and life-altering. In an instant, a wave of peace flooded over me coupled with an unmistakable feeling of belonging. In a gentle sort of parting of the veil of time, I saw, or more aptly felt, my own passing someday, and I knew I would die here someday in the distant future in the Land of Enchantment. To be clear, I did not see the specifics or the details, and it wouldn't happen anytime soon. Nor had I ever pondered such a thing, but in that brief moment on the highway, I saw the feeling of it and it was beauty-filled. It came with a sense of pure comfort and completeness, something that I had longed for my whole life. In a strange state of surrender, a wave of knowingness came over me mixed with a rare feeling that "all is well and will be well in the universe." It left me unafraid and awake to the hunch that I was mysteriously and unexpectedly coming into alignment with my right place and right life.

Liberated from the clutter of daily life and modern thinking, I was reduced to bare essentials and freed to sink into the question of what really matters after the storm. It was refreshing to wake before dawn and drive into Santa Fe watching the sun rise over the Sangre de Cristo Mountains while listening to Josh Groban's "The Prayer." So beautiful, so exquisite, sometimes, all I could do was cry, and often, I would have to pull over and call my mom. Longing for someone to share it with, to bear witness to this wonder of life, I would narrate via cell phone from my car. Together, on this mountainous edge of daybreak, we would take in the birth of day, in awe as deep purple emerged to outline the horizon and then burst into a sky flooded in azure and crimson. Heading to Starbucks to use the Internet when they opened at 6 a.m. became an ordinary yet extraordinary adventure. The flow of humanity coming in and out for coffee became a crucible of new connections, story-sharing, and unexpected community-weaving.

Extricated through disaster from the habits of regular life, existence was no longer mundane. I could not take anything for granted anymore, and with senses acute, I began feeling alive in a way I had not felt in a long time. Paying keen attention to everything, I woke daily with a sense of wonder and gratitude that made the simplest of things more precious and delightful than ever before. As the grace of living became more and more alive, I watched synchronicity rise and my path begin to reveal itself.

In the midst of all the upheaval, my mom was diagnosed with lung cancer and miraculously, caught so early, she went through a sudden and unexpected surgery and fully recovered without need of chemo or radiation (another blessing and miracle story). As she stabilized, and my parents sunk into life as refugees in my sister's guest-room in Mississippi, I made a decision to follow my gut feeling and give New Mexico a try. So, in the new year, I flew West and started a whole new life from scratch.

Within a week of landing, I was standing in the pre-dawn darkness of winter at the San Ildefonso Pueblo bundled in a blanket and watching the Buffalo dancers come over the mountain as the sun rose behind them, singing and praying their way into the village as the community lined the way to greet them, elders and infants alike, wrapped in rainbow-colored Pendletons. In that moment and in that sunrise, and many more since, you could taste the eternal and feel the integrity of creation, and your place in it, in a way that leaves you humble and happy. It is a sense of peace and belonging that is beyond words but weans you instantly of worry and hurry and flurry and longing. In this state of grace, amazing things happened, even at Starbucks. I made lifelong friends and even met my future husband, who first showed up in plaid flannel pajamas drinking coffee and conversing with a handful of the "coffee-people," as they have lovingly come to be known.

Over coffee in DeVargas mall one morning, while sitting in what I now fondly refer to as one of the "magic chairs," a conversation ensued with a Dine' educator that changed my life forever. After learning I was a refugee from Katrina, he asserted that I was in "root shock," and my whole being was rocked to the core. Like plants that go into shock when they are removed from the earth and relocated, humans, he asserted, can go through the same dangerous, debilitating, and even potentially deadly trauma when uprooted. I knew instantly he was telling the truth. This knowing launched a profound journey of restoration and healing that was further catalyzed by the simple yet profound words of wisdom he added, "Well-being is nourished by being accountable to a people and a place." Yes. These words have since shaped my entire life and work. In the nomadic modern world, human "root shock" may be pandemic for many reasons. In my case, spurred by an unexpected natural disaster, for one simple human in search of a meaningful and responsible life, the invitation to re-rooting became a blessing of epic proportion.

The process took me deep into the exploration of what it means to create a life worth living and what it means to live a life of well-being and balance. What matters has turned out to be far simpler than expensive suits and rushing through traffic to work. The lessons are vivid and still obvious here, in the spectacular and still vibrant wonder of nature and in the traditional Native and Spanish families and communities that have lived here in the same exact place for many centuries and in some cases, hundreds of generations. With simplicity and gratitude, the invisible graces of life have revealed themselves, and the simple riches of human existence that come from relationship, family, and real community, from belonging, connection, and meaningful work, proved an extraordinary and deeply nourishing gift.

Meanwhile, my life-work evolved, and I began a small, local non-profit called Community Learning Network, dedicated to "building community through real-life learning in real-life places with real-life people." Grounded in the principles of sustainability, resiliency, and community-based learning, our initiatives are designed to celebrate what there is to learn and to love about where we live, work, and play. We celebrate the amazing people and projects all around us, here in our own home. We reweave our community by reconnecting future generations with the preceding ones. Creating a life worth living, I am blessed to know and work with a vast array of humble yet amazing humans doing amazing things here in northern New Mexico. I'm blessed to share this with our future generations. It is not only rewarding, it is just plain fun.

Over a decade has passed since the storm came ashore in 2005. Prior to the storm, life was spent racing through days of hustle and bustle in big cities like San Diego, Los Angeles, and Washington DC. Life was struggling through traffic to travel a few miles in an hour or two on highways with sometimes twelve or more lanes and wearing expensive, designer suits while scrambling to find meaning through a range of work in big organizations. My life now is completely different than I could have ever imaged back then.

Now, I live in the desert and wear jeans and cowboy boots almost every day. Most of what I need to tend to in town is within a five-minute radius either walking or driving, and in fifteen minutes I am enjoying stunning hiking trails steeped in the unadulterated majesty, magic, and medicine of nature in all her glory. Moreover, I have been blessed to spend thousands of hours out on the land learning from the traditional people here where the pace of human existence remains slow and determined, uncrushed and still faithful to values that elsewhere seem to be cracking under the weight of modernity. I am grateful to live in a place where it's not uncommon to know your neighbors and where people still stop to talk to one another and go out their way for each other, where elders and children and water and clean air matter.

Since the hurricane, everything has changed. Everything has slowed down. Everything has grown deeper, simpler, richer, more full. Although there have been new twists and turns and challenges since the hurricane turned my previous life completely upside down, I have been blessed with an extensive new circle of characters to cherish as "family," and life is full and rich with what our beloved and inspiring niece calls "all the lovin and eatin." Friends and family touch our lives daily and waking up is an exciting adventure. The little things of daily life and the wealth of relationships are precious and now give profound strength and vitality to the fabric of my existence. I feel a sense of purpose and place and accountability and belonging like never before. I am grateful to live into the responsibility of my own humanity while sinking into the web of life and community that is still alive and well here in the "Land of Enchantment" that is my home.

PART 3: TOOLS FOR NAVIGATING AN UNEXPECTED AWAKENING

CHAPTER 19

SEEKING HELP AND SUPPORT

Most of my clients find me somewhere between Stage Two (Intervention/Reorganization) and Stage Three (Liminal/Still Point) of their unexpected awakening experience. Sometimes I'll get a client at the initiation of their crisis moment, but typically they find their way toward alternative methods, like energy work, after they have already entered Stage Two and have exhausted other modalities to address their crisis. Sometimes, too, they have found their way through the crisis and into new ways of being, but are in the liminal stage and are looking for what they need to *do* next. For many doers, that liminal stage is actually more challenging than walking through the fire of transformation itself.

This section is dedicated to offering my thoughts and ideas for how to navigate the awakening experience. I've asked each of the contributors to provide a list of resources that helped them along the way, that they wished they'd known about, or had during their awakening experience. This list is included under the Contributors' Resource Recommendations. By no means is this meant to be an exhaustive list, to be *one size fits all,* or to speak to everyone who reads this book. It's simply our best attempt at providing some signposts that you may find helpful as you find what works best for you.

The very nature of the awakening experience, as hopefully you've come to find by now, is extremely unique to the person experiencing it. When I work with a new client, I meet them where they are at, and tailor a course of work that is ever-changing based on their particular needs. In this same way, your journey through your awakening will be specific to you and your individual path.

That journey truly *is* the awakening. It's so much less about the end result, although it certainly feels nice to meet life from a more authentic, balanced, and peaceful place. What you'll discover about yourself through the process of awakening is the gold you'll be mining for the rest of your life. There can be a beautiful gift of excitement as you embark on the beginner's journey. Remember to come back there whenever you feel lost, regardless of how long you may have been journeying and into the next stages of your awakening.

The awakening experience is naturally a lonely one. Most of us find an organic inclination to withdraw, to be on our own, to pull away from people and places, so we can find our way to still point. Honoring this tendency and desire is paramount, and at the same time, it is important to find even just one teacher, guide, or friend who can help hold your hand as you move through the process.

People go through awakenings by themselves all the time, but the one piece of feedback I hear consistently from those who did is, "I wish I had found someone to help me out sooner," or, "It would have been so helpful to know I wasn't alone, that I wasn't the only person going through this." This type of commentary partially inspired the birth of this book.

I personally believe we all find our way to the people who are meant to help us at exactly the right time. In that same vein, I believe you are reading these words about seeking help and support at exactly the time you need to read them.

Some of us find that having a dedicated teacher, practitioner or guide is all that we need. For others, the awakening process includes a full team of teachers and practitioners, as well as new friends and community. Again, your experience is unique to you, so allow yourself to do what feels right and good to you.

Professionals

As a member of this group, I have a natural bias toward finding a practitioner of some kind to help you through your awakening. You want to be sure that whoever you are working with is trained, with experience, in a healing modality, and has the tools, background, and education to help navigate you through your experience.

Within our current self-help, self-professed guru society, almost anyone can hang a shingle and call themselves a "healer," or "coach" without any formal certifications or training. While some of the best healers I have seen in other parts of the world had zero certification, they did have a deep and rich shamanic and cultural tradition that prepared them to do healing work.

Having gone through an awakening process does not a professional practitioner make. Unfortunately, I have seen many clients put their trust and faith in a practitioner who either wasn't the right fit for them or didn't have the qualifications and experience that the particular individual needed. Spend some time thinking about your past, your issues, and your personal style. It's okay to interview anyone you may want to work with, and this may look like needing to pay for one initial session. You should never feel pressured into buying packages or signing up for classes or work before you've had the chance to engage with the person you'll be working with.

Read their website or blog, check out their videos or social media channels. Look at their credentials and maybe even send an email asking a few clarifying questions if needed. You'll want to be respectful of their time, but also, trusting someone with your mental, emotional, and spiritual health is a deep commitment. If something doesn't feel right during your session, trust your gut. Either ask more questions and share that with the person you're working with in an effort to better understand what's happening, or don't be ashamed to walk away and try someone else.

I am not a fit for everyone that comes through my door. I usually trust that by the time they've made their way to me, something larger than us both has guided them there. There certainly have been times I've worked with someone and they haven't returned. I am able to check my ego enough to not make that about me, and to honor them for doing what felt right for them.

Depending on the type of modality you are comfortable with, this is a non-exhaustive list of the types of professionals whose help you may seek:

- Acupuncturists/Chinese doctors, Ayurvedic doctors, and Alternative/Eastern Medicine practitioners
- Bodyworkers and massage therapists
- Energy workers (i.e. Reiki, pranic healing, healing touch, cranial sacral therapy, etc.)
- Priests, priestesses, monks, nuns, and other types of spiritual/intuitive counselors
- Life and career coaches
- Therapists, social workers, and counselors (Ph.D.s, MFTs, LCSWs, etc.)

New Community

When you're ready, you may find that you want to expand your community to include others who have journeyed through similar awakening experiences. As part of your awakening, you may find yourself naturally gravitating to new activities and/or experiences in a new community.

Finding a spiritual tradition that resonates with you can also be extremely helpful. While your awakening may not be spiritual in nature, I have found that an element of the spiritual is contained in most awakenings. Finding a connection to a spiritual tradition that resonates with you may help you find community so you can make the best sense out of your process.

Family and Friends

Family can be a double-edged sword for many during the awakening experience. For most of us, some type of distancing from family members tends to be natural as we seek a new version of ourselves. It can be hard to rebirth the self while inside of the very system that is responsible for most of the hardwiring of the old self. We usually distance ourselves from certain family members and/or friends at different times during our awakening trajectory. It's also not uncommon to want to distance from family members with whom we had been closest; this, indeed, can be one of the more distressing parts of the awakening. Family and friends who we are used to feeling so close to, and relying on for support, suddenly feel annoying, upsetting, and/or frustrating, and we find we have a difficult time being around them.

This typically passes, but it's exacerbated when we try to push ourselves back into the old types of relationships, instead of honoring that desire for space so that something new can emerge.

CHAPTER 20

INDUCING STILL POINT

From my personal and professional perspective, I find that inducing still point (Stage Three) is absolutely key to any healing process, and certainly to the awakening experience. Inducing still point necessarily includes surrender, finding your way toward non-attachment, and creating time and space for your awakening to occur.

Awakenings and healing can't be forced. When we try and force them, we simply get more of the same: more friction, more pain, and more confusion. In yoga we talk about breathing into the asana or pose, leaning into the pain and discomfort (without hurting or damaging) until it gradually begins to subside. As Carl Jung stated, "What you resist not only persists, but will grow in size."

Below are suggestions to help you find your way to still point, so that you can process and work through your awakening. No matter what stage you are at in the experience, still point can always be beneficial as it creates time to rest and digest, while you are processing your experience.

- Art/music; Engaging Your Creativity

- Body Work
- Breathwork
- Journaling
- Meditation
- Time in Nature and Nature Activities
- Resting
- Self-Care Activities
- Vacation and Travel
- Yoga, Chi Gong & Tai Chi

QUESTIONS FOR SELF-REFLECTION

Engaging the rational mind in reflection around your awakening process can be an extremely helpful exercise in understanding where you've been and where you're going. While much of the awakening process is geared toward engaging non-linear types of thinking, for most of us, the awakening process becomes a little less scary and more tangible when we spend some time working with the rational mind to understand the journey we are embarking upon.

I've included below a few key questions you may consider exploring as you look at your transformation.

1. What fueled your awakening? What events (crises?) propelled your awakening into action?
2. What choices led you here? What might have you done differently?
3. What habits, behaviors, relationships and/or thought patterns (beliefs) are you wanting to let go of? What might you need to do in order to let these go?
4. What are the pain points? Which ones are the most challenging and

what help do you need working through them?

5. What are the benefits?

6. Who are you becoming?

7. What victories can you already begin to celebrate?

8. How can you use this awakening to propel your self-growth?

9. Where do you want your life to go from here?

Awakening Timeline Exercise

I've found through the process of writing this book, and compiling the stories within, that there is something cathartic about writing about the awakening journey. At the onset of writing this book, we had about twice the number of contributors that we ended up publishing. It was understood when folks committed that life might change and they may need to bow out.

Everyone who participated gained something vital from the process of even just opening the lid on the container of their awakening process. I've included below the timeline exercise that was shared with the contributors in the event you may want to do a timeline exercise for yourself.

Awakening Timeline Instructions

Creating a personal timeline will be the first step in understanding the depth and trajectory of the awakening journey, and also helps to understand where you may hone in. You can use whatever format you'd like, but the key is capturing important/formative dates and events in your life. These events include moving, travel, relationships, family shifts and changes, friendships, marriages and divorces, health issues, personal crises, spiritual development and personal growth.

Sample grid:

Event/Experience	Date	Reflections on Importance in My Life

Once you've outlined these key events and experiences, circle or star those that pop out as being particularly significant or juicy. You may even want to free write about the events, focusing on how you felt, who was with you, what your reactions or responses were to the events, as well as the reactions of those around you. How did you feel and what did you think before, during, and after? What were the takeaways, the gold that you mined through this process?

Owning how far you've come, consolidating or synthesizing what you've learned and how you've grown can be a wonderful way of celebrating your victories as well as identifying areas that are still raw or painful which may highlight places of future growth and healing.

CHAPTER 21

EDUCATIONAL RESOURCES

Educating yourself can be an extremely empowering and valuable way of deepening your awakening experience. I've included below some of my favorite resources, as well as those of our contributors. In order to help keep the list relevant and longer than what is publishable here, you can also visit unexpectedawakenings.com for an ongoing and updated list.

Classes & Workshops

Attending in-person and/or online classes and workshops can be extremely helpful as you navigate your awakening experience. Not only can you learn important new tools and skills to help you understand yourself and your transformation better, these are places where you may encounter new friends and community. Many people find that a class or workshop itself is the propulsion into an awakening.

- Healing arts courses and certifications
- Health and wellness courses and certifications
- Movement classes and workshops (i.e. yoga, tai chi, chi gong, etc.)

- Meditation classes and retreats
- Personal development workshops & retreats
- Psychology, social work and activisms courses and degrees

Books, Blogs, Videos & Podcasts

So much information is available online, as well as via traditional book format. Searching for topics of interest to you and your awakening can often yield some incredible information. Again, there is so much more of value and worth than I could list here, but some of my favorite books are included below.

AUTHOR'S BOOK RECOMMENDATIONS

Science of Energy Medicine

- *Hands of Light*, Barbara Brennan
- *The Biology of Belief*, Dr. Bruce Lipton
- *The Field*, Lynne McTaggart
- *Human Tuning Sound Healing with Tuning Forks*, John Beaulieu
- *Psychic Protection: Creating Positive Energies For People and Places*, William Bloom

Spirituality & the Awakening Process

- *Kundalini Rising*, Gurmukh Kaur Khalsa, Dorothy Walters
- *Comfortable with Uncertainty* and *When Things Apart*, Pema Chodron
- *The Untethered Soul: The Journey Beyond Yourself*, Michael Singer
- *Druid Priestess* and *Kissing the Hag*, Emma Restall Orr
- *No Mud, No Lotus* and *Peace is Every Breath*, Thich Nhat Hanh
- *Spiral Dance*, Starhawk
- *The Four Agreements*, Don Miguel Ruiz
- The works of Martín Prechtel

Past Lives and the Other Side

- *Journey of Souls*, Dr. Michael Newton
- *Adventures of the Soul*, James Van Praagh
- *How to Hear Your Angels*, Doreen Virtue
- *Conversations with God*, Neale Donald Walsch

Changing Thought Patterns/Beliefs

- *The Gifts of Imperfection* and *Daring Greatly*, Dr. Brené Brown
- *Dark Side of the Light Chasers*, Debbie Ford
- *The Power of Intention* and *Pulling Your Own Strings*, Dr. Wayne Dyer
- *A Return to Love: Reflections on the Principles of "A Course in Miracles"*, Marianne Williamson
- *The Empath's Survival Guide* and *Positive Energy and Emotional Freedom*, Judith Orloff, MD
- *Hand Me Down Blues*, Dr. Michael Yapko
- *Radical Forgiveness and Radical Self Forgiveness*, Colin Tipping
- *White Hot Truth*, Danielle LaPorte
- *Loving Yourself to Great Health*, Louise Hay, Ahlea Khadro, Heather Dane

CONTRIBUTORS RESOURCE RECOMMENDATIONS

Below is a list of each of the contributors in order of appearance in the book and the tools and resources that either helped them navigate their awakening process, and/or that they discovered and wished they'd know about at the time. If a particular author's story resonated with you, it may be helpful to also look at the supports and systems they recommend.

Juliet Erickson ("Grace")

- *The Miracle of Mindfulness: An Introduction into the Practice of Meditation*,

Thich Nhat Hanh.

- Compassion Cultivation Training. 8 week course. Compassion Institute, Stanford University
- 1 week Silent Meditation Retreat, Center for Mindful Self-Compassion, Berkeley, CA
- Reiki treatments and Reiki 1 Certification
- Tonglen Meditation
- Taking vacations and dinner dates with just myself
- Walking generally and walking in nature as often as possible
- Sitting alone without digital distraction
- Regular daily pauses for gratefulness
- Random acts of kindness
- Yoga

Beverly McDonald ("Courage")

- *The Four Agreements,* Don Miguel Ruiz
- "Anxiety Slayer" podcast
- "The Positive Head" podcast
- *The Alchemist,* Paulo Coelho
- Breathing techniques, specifically learning how to take diaphragmatic breathing and toning

J. Whitley ("Transitions")

- Life coach
- Mentor
- Courses on confidence

JR MacGregor ("Forgiveness")

- *You Can Heal Your Life*, Louise Hay
- *Love Yourself* and *Heal Your Life Workbook*, Louise Hay
- *Love Warrior*, Glennon Doyle Melton
- *The Shift* (movie), Dr. Wayne Dyer
- *White Hot Truth*, Danielle LaPorte

Lynn Kay ("Faith)

- *Return to Love*, Marianne Williamson
- Landmark Education, The Forum 3-day event
- *Know you Know*, Ashan
- *Emmanuel's Book III*, Pat Rodegast & Judith Stanton
- *God on a Harley*, Joan Brady
- Notes from the Universe, TUT.com

Samantha Bishop ("Rebirth")

- Yoga
- Solo walks in the woods
- *Reveal*, Meggan Watterson
- *The Journey*, Brandon Bays
- Five YouTube Interview Symposium by Liz DiAlto
- Reiki Certification
- "Symptoms of an Awakening" article on TheAwakenedState.net
- *Trust Your Vibes*, Sonia Choquette

Caroline Smith ("Self-Love")

- *When Things Fall Apart*, Pema Chodron
- *The Untethered Soul: The Journey Beyond Yourself*, Michael A. Singer
- Starting therapy earlier in life

- Local women's support group
- Reiki shares

Rose Gibson ("Empowerment")

- Abraham-Hicks
- Hay House authors and podcasts
- *The Book of Love & Creation*, Paul Selig
- Feng shui
- Meditation
- Shamanism and Earth-based spiritual practices

Katy Hughes ("Awareness")

- *Radical Forgiveness*, Colin Tipping
- *The Power of Now: A Guide to Spiritual Enlightenment*, Eckhart Tolle
- *The Untethered Soul: The Journey Beyond Yourself*, Michael A. Singer
- *The Four Agreements: A Practical Guide to Personal Freedom*, Don Miguel Ruiz
- *The Fifth Agreement: A Practical Guide to Self-Mastery*, Don Miguel Ruiz & Don Jose Ruiz
- *Miracles at Work: Turning Inner Guidance into Outer Influence*, Emily Bennington

Lauren Lenore ("Surrender")

- *When Things Fall Apart*, Pema Chodron
- *Conversations with God*, Neale Donald Walsch
- *The Top Ten Things Dead People Want to Tell You*, Mike Dooley
- Living in Divine Balance Online Course
- *The Magic*, Rhonda Byrne
- Reiki 1 Certification

- Meditation in Everyday Life Course with the Shambhala Center Portland
- *On Being* with Krista Tippet Podcast

Jennifer Nevarez ("Renewal")

- Walks and time in nature
- Prayer, stillness, and quiet time
- Crayons and markers for drawing
- Music, especially "Humble and Kind" by Tim McGraw, "The Prayer," by Josh Groban and The Dixie Chicks
- *My Name is Chellis and I am in Recovery from Western Civilization*, Chellis Glendinning

CONCLUSION

Nearly a year ago, eighteen smiling faces looked out at me from my computer screen, excitedly saying hello to me and to one another before we began our first video conference call. I was nervous, feeling the anticipation of this Awakenings Book Project. Wanting to steward the endeavor well, I felt the responsibility of the trust they had placed in me by agreeing to tell their stories. The video conference format allowed me to see a Hollywood Squares-tile version of these incredible individuals. As I scanned their faces, I was flooded with the memory of working with each person for the first time.

It was a montage affect as my eyes landed on each one: my vision sparkled with flashes of their journeys and healing paths. While I didn't work with all of them during their awakening process, I know their stories and what they've been through. I was in awe of the force of power that came across the screen through the combination of their wisdom, strength, bravery, and growth. I still am.

The stories you've read are by someone who has struggled, likely as you or a loved one is or has. Reflecting on this first assembly of these courageous and magnificent individuals, many of whom had never met one another before, I'm reminded that the beginning of a project is also a perfect place for its conclusion. The beginning becomes the ending becomes another beginning, just like the awakening process. This cycle also underscores another vital theme: community.

The loneliness that is inherent during an unexpected awakening is one of its most difficult components. Having concrete tools to understand and navigate the process is key to surviving it. But to thrive within an awakening requires reaching out, finding a stronghold of someone or many someones who can help you along the way.

As a species, we're not built to navigate life alone, and yet we live during a time when most of us feel that we must shoulder life's challenges nearly, if not entirely, on our own. Independence, strength, perseverance, and certainty have been deeply ingrained into many of us since childhood. Because these are exactly the qualities the awakening process shatters as we are forced to surrender, we must ask for help and seek out community.

The tools and stories in this book are meant to contribute to this process of seeking support. Hopefully you've seen just how unique and varied the crisis moment(s) that beget(s) an awakening can be, in addition to how unique and varied the process of awakening is. While there are similarities in the journey, what makes an unexpected awakening both beautiful and horrible is that it will always be distinct to the person going through it.

I've found that those who seek out community of some kind during their awakening suffer the least. While it's true that finding community can itself be the source of suffering, this too produces its own lessons and growth. As you come to understand who you truly are, you're better able to attract relationships that fit you best. If you do find yourself in a place of searching for community to no avail, please visit UnexpectedAwakenings.com where we'll endeavor to help you locate a local or virtual community.

I'm also finding that the personal crises that prompt the unexpected awakening process mirror the crises that we are experiencing as a collective. It only takes a simple browsing of news headlines, anywhere in the world, to see that we are living in polarizing, destructive, and uncertain times. I believe this is also why so many more people are waking up now at an increasingly accelerated rate, in what feels like droves. As a result, many don't know where to turn, and/or don't have the language to describe what they're going through, much less the resources to understand it. An unexpected awakening, by its nature, is uncomfortable, scary, and confusing.

Moreover, traditional forms of personal development work don't always address the larger spiritual and collective concerns of an awakening. We make what could be a spiritual, community-driven process into something secular and isolated, rooted solely in the practical, personal human experience: we distill crisis moments down to the What and When, rather than the Why and How. In doing so, we isolate people from a larger context that might provide them with a sense of wholeness, unity, and connection to something greater than themselves and their own personal experience. For many, after the awakening crisis has subsided, a sense of stability ensues, along with a compulsion to use their new knowledge to help others, contributing to a larger awakening movement that is happening across the planet.

If we are to survive not only our own awakening process, but also thrive as a species and a planet, we need one another and we need purpose. We are built to search for connection, to question why we are here, and once we awaken, we almost always feel compelled to use our gifts and skills in a meaningful way. For many of us, the spiritual component of the awakening is how we tie together a sense of purpose in helping others and contributing to the advancement of the collective good. For others, spirituality as a framework is less important, but perhaps they feel a sense of connection to science as a way to make sense of the awakening and their need to find purpose. Either way, we live in a vast, mysterious universe, and it's inarguable that we are tiny pieces of an enormous cosmos that we know relatively little about.

Waking up allows us to connect to these mysteries in a deeper way and forces us to be present along an unfolding path in which we balance responsibility and participation with surrender and acceptance of the unknown. When we also balance self-reflection, awareness, and personal development with connection to community and others, we ensure a better future for ourselves and the planet. For me, this is the entire purpose of the awakening process: to be more happy and at peace inside oneself, as well as coming together as a collective for the greater good.

My hope is this book makes some small contribution in this arena and reminds us, as Ram Dass so beautifully writes, that "we are all just walking each other home."

ACKNOWLEDGMENTS

The largest acknowledgement must of course go to the contributors to this book: the brave individuals who agreed to jump aboard ship with me on this project when I really had no idea what I was doing. They so authentically and completely showed up in every way requested of them, and additionally in ways I never thought imaginable. They had patience with me as I learned alongside them. Most importantly, they were willing to unpack and revisit times in their lives that were incredibly painful, intense, and complex.

Their stories make up the heart and soul of this book. These individuals are also the deepest guiding inspiration to me, and some of my most profound teachers. Many have chosen to write under pen names, to preserve their privacy and that of those included in the stories.

Thank you Beverly McDonald, Caroline Smith, J. Whitely, Jennifer Nevarez, JR MacGregor, Juliet Erickson, Katy Hughes, Lauren Lenore, Lynn Kay, Rose Gibson and Samantha Bishop.

I'd also like to acknowledge all the incredible individuals who initially signed up for this project. I was overwhelmed by the response from clients and students who wanted to share their stories. I was blown away by how the writing process created catharsis for those involved, regardless of whether or not they ultimately decided to contribute to the book. It underscored what I know to be true: that the process is so much more important than the outcome, and that often, the process itself changes the initial, envisioned outcome.

Tanya MacIntosh, you are a goddess in the highest sense of the word. Thank you for your incredible editing work on this book, without which it would be a tumbling around of words (mainly mine!). Your gentleness and care in lovingly holding each story was felt by all involved, and we are so grateful for your ability to shape each contributor's words in a way that held their voice and amplified it to an even higher level.

Beth Moutrey, your beautiful artwork is a gift to each story and to the cover. Thank you for beautifully capturing each person's story and the book's vision with your skill, talent and spirit. I'm so grateful to know you.

I'm also grateful for those who have provided feedback, expertise and support of this book including Daniel Caleb, Lynne Grove Avalon, Elizabeth Holthe, Lisa Langlais, Phil Langlais, Stephanie and Andrew Lee, Jennifer Nevarez, Kathy Sebuck, and Melissa Stynes. Thank you for your wisdom, love, kindness and support.

Thank you to each client and student who I've had the honor to work with, whose experiences have helped shape this book, as well as the friends, acquaintances and random encounters that have done the same.

Finally, thank you to each person reading this book, as well as each person who is making a commitment to improving personally at this vitally important moment in time.

Your grace, courage, and work benefits us all.

ABOUT THE AUTHOR
SHARNA LANGLAIS

Working with clients internationally, Sharna helps them uncover the source of wounds and blockages in their pursuit of living freer, fuller, and brighter lives. Using Reiki, meditation, and energy therapy, she facilitates a holistic and individualized journey toward healing. Sharna is a Certified Reiki Master, Certified Say It Straight Communication Trainer, Certified Herbalist (360 Hour Clinical Program), and Certified Aromatherapist. Sharna also writes articles for MindBodyGreen, Elephant Journal, and Rebelle Society. Sharna maintains an in-person practice in Santa Fe, NM and San Diego, CA, and travels internationally to work with clients and teach classes. Her online classes are offered on a regular basis, along with Reiki Certifications, and private, telephone, and in-person Reiki & Intuitive Healing sessions.

SeekSparkShine.com
UnexpectedAwakenings.com

@sharnalanglais
#UnexpectedAwakenings

Photo credit: Elizabeth Craig Photography

NOTES

[1] Pinkola Estés Ph.D., Clarissa, *Women Who Run with the Wolves* (New York: Ballantine Books, 1996), 15.

[2] Dorothy Walters, Ph.D., "Kundalini and the Mystic Path," ed. Gurmukh Kaur Khalsa, et al., *Kundalini Rising: Exploring the Energy of Awakening* (Boulder: Sounds True, 2009), 9.

[3] Underhill, Evelyn, *Mysticism: A Study in the Nature and Development of Spiritual Consciousness* (Mineola: Dover Publications, 2002).

[4] St. John of the Cross, *The Poems of St. John of the Cross* (Chicago: University of Chicago Press, 1995).

[5] Beaulieu, John, *Human Tuning: Sound Healing with Tuning Forks* (Stone Ridge: BioSonic Enterprises, Ltd, 2010), 17-23.

[6] Jenny, MD., Hans, *Cymatics: A Study of Wave Phenomena & Vibration* (Macromedia, 2001).

[7] Beaulieu, John, *Human Tuning: Sound Healing with Tuning Forks* (Stone Ridge: BioSonic Enterprises, Ltd, 2010), 21-22.

[8] Taken in part from Dorothy Walters, Ph.D., "Kundalini and the Mystic Path," ed. Gurmukh Kaur Khalsa, et al., *Kundalini Rising: Exploring the Energy of Awakening* (Boulder: Sounds True, 2009), 17. And crimsoncircle.com/documents/Twelve%20Awakening%20Signs.pdf

[9] Dorothy Walters, Ph.D., "Kundalini and the Mystic Path," ed. Gurmukh Kaur Khalsa, et al., *Kundalini Rising: Exploring the Energy of Awakening* (Boulder: Sounds True, 2009), 13-15.

[10] Jung, Carl G., *Man and His Symbols* (New York: Dell Publishing Company, Inc., 1968).

[11] Jung, Carl G., *Man and His Symbols* (New York: Dell Publishing Company, Inc., 1968).

[12] Richard A. Rogers, "From Cultural Exchange to Transculturation: A Review and Reconceptualization of Cultural Appropriation," (2006). doi.org/10.1111/j.1468-2885.2006.00277.x